*Asghar Farhadi*

# Asghar Farhadi

*Life and Cinema*

Tina Hassannia

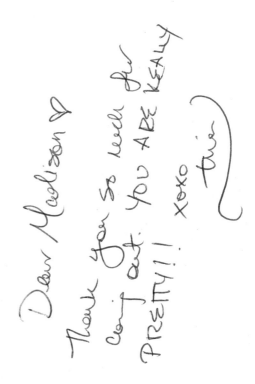

The Critical Press
Raleigh, NC

Copyright © 2014 by Tina Hassannia
Rights Reserved
Printed in the United States of America

Hassannia, Tina.
Asghar Farhadi : life and cinema / Tina Hassannia.
pages cm
Includes bibliographical references and index.
LCCN 2014953084
ISBN 978-1-941629-02-4 (pbk.)
ISBN 978-1-941629-03-1 (electronic bk. text)

1. Farhādī, Aṣghar, 1972—Criticism and interpretation. 2. Motion picture producers and directors–Iran. 3. Screenwriters–Iran.  I. Title.

PN1998.3.F36H37 2014        791.4302'3092
QBI14-600173

*To Calum and McLuhan*

# Contents

| | |
|---|---|
| Acknowledgements | ix |
| Introduction | 1 |
| Interview | 5 |
| *Dancing in the Dust*<br>Shattered Glass | 29 |
| *Beautiful City*<br>Do the Right Thing | 39 |
| *Fireworks Wednesday*<br>The Day I Became A Woman | 49 |
| *About Elly*<br>Secrets and Lies | 61 |
| *A Separation*<br>Divorce Iranian Style | 69 |
| *The Past*<br>An Iranian in Paris | 79 |
| Notes | 89 |
| Bibliography | 97 |
| Index | 101 |
| About the Author | 103 |

## Acknowledgements

This book would not have been possible without the following people:

I'd like to thank Tom Elrod, my editor at The Critical Press, for giving me the opportunity to write my first book. It's only the beginnings for this new publishing company, but I trust it will become a huge success. I must also thank Tom for letting me write about my favorite national cinema and one of my favorite filmmakers. And on the subject of Mr. Asghar Farhadi, I'd like to thank him for generously answering my questions, for his films, and for giving our culture's cinema a new voice. He was patient, generous with his time, and hospitable enough to let me speak English (as my Farsi is not the greatest). I must also credit his publicist, Ms. Samin Mohajerani, for being an invaluable source in organizing the interviews and getting all the information I needed.

Thanks to friends and family for their moral support as I delved into what seemed like an impossible project. To Sam Fragoso, Colin Waterman, Laura White, Tim Robertson, Diana Barboza, Goldie, Miranda Hunt, Kumru Bilici, Hisham Kelati, Jason Chiu, Wassim Garzouzi, Dan Schindel, my cinephile Twitter circle, and many other friends who kept me on an even keel, even when I felt like giving up.

I couldn't have overcome my lack of confidence to finish this project without the support of Dr. John Wachsmuth, who helps me conquer my ADHD one day at a time. To all the writers whose reviews helped me shape my own opinions on these films, and giving me the pleasure of reading illuminating film criticism. To the patient, ever-loving friends I couldn't spend time with for the past six months, and whom I'll have to win back in the months to come.

To my translators—Ted Scheinman, Alex Huls, and Liz Thompson—for all their hard work and for trusting in my promise to one day pay them back with beer. To Behnaz Beigui, my talented photographer, who was able to make me look as beautiful as I possibly can. I couldn't have accomplished anything in this book without the help of my resourceful friend Amir Soltani, who helped me every step of the way, navigating Persian sources, diligently translating them, answering my every question about

Iranian culture, giving me a multitude of great ideas, and serving as my interpreter during interviews.

And to Calum: for loving me, supporting me, and putting up with me, even in my most dour moments. I don't know why or how I was blessed with such an amazing partner, but somehow he's managed to stick by me for nearly six years. I couldn't have done this without him, or our cat for that matter, Marshall McLuhan, who sat dotingly by my side as I wrote, giving me love bites, and keeping me company at all hours of the night.

Finally, thanks to my beloved family. To my sister Diana and brother-in-law Bob, for believing in me. To Mum and Dad, for helping me track down sources in Iran, teaching me to have pride in our cultural heritage, patiently answering my questions and always encouraging my curiosity.

# Introduction

> Today morality is an awkward word associated with genuflections and fairy tales, prejudices and superstitions. Morality is concealed from ourselves, either out of convenience or coercion. The persistent and patient reflection required by true morality is unfashionable in some places, punishable in others. Yet it is there in all our thoughts and actions. It permeates our expectations and emotions. It is the language of self-identity. The first step to the rediscovery of morality, a terribly difficult one, is to see its reality, to appreciate its weight and to acknowledge its complexity. – Joseph Burke[1]

Since the late 1980s, when a small group of American film critics began to discover hidden gems coming out of Iran, the state, quality, and reception of this national cinema has remained a contentious topic. This is perhaps due to one obvious fact: Iran's relationship with the rest of the world (particularly the West) has remained mostly hostile since the 1980s, and cinema has become a useful medium in offering a small glimpse into this occluded, foreign culture. That look is an image at odds with the evil fundamentalists Iranians are so regularly portrayed as being in the media. Thanks to the well-regarded works of Iranian auteurs like Abbas Kiarostami, Mohsen Makhmalbaf, Jafar Panahi, and others, people have come to understand the humanist tendencies in Iranian culture, the society's contradictions, its deeply rooted flaws and pleasures, the injustices the government forces onto its repressed citizens, its language (both verbal and physical), Iran's traditions and customs, and the different faces and identities of Iranians.

For the past several years, fewer quality Iranian works have found distribution and won awards abroad compared to Iranian cinema's golden era of the 1990s. In 2013, Hamid Dabashi argued that due to a brain drain driven by government censorship, Iranian cinema could be slowly dying: "The ruling regime in Iran has succeeded in ripping the leading Iranian filmmakers from the fabric of their society and cast them into vague and ambiguous environments about which they know very little."[2]

In his piece, Dabashi fails to describe how Iranian cinema actually operates inside the country, seeming to imply that Iran's only useful cinematic output is its artistic films. In Iran, like other national cinemas, there are two distinct types of film. One is the auteur-driven, arthouse cinema that appeals to Western cinephiles and is frequently dismissed by domestic audiences and the government.[3] This cinema constitutes a small fraction of the number of films being made in Iran. The other type is called the "main-body cinema," and is decidedly more commercial, encompassing melodramas, comedies, and other genres that speak more broadly to mainstream Iranian audiences. For the most part, these films have not made waves abroad. And few directors have been able to bridge the gap between arthouse and the main-body cinema.

Asghar Farhadi—the most successful Iranian filmmaker inside and outside of the country—is one proven, undeniable exception to this rule, and he's claimed that mainstream approval from his homeland has always been an integral goal for him. Part of the reason Farhadi has been able to so deftly incorporate both mainstream appeal and artistic value in his work is due to his varied artistic background, which includes experience and training in not only filmmaking, but mediums that range from high to low-brow: theater, television, and radio.

Farhadi, born in 1972 and raised in Isfahan, became intensely interested in cinema from a young age. As a teenager he made several short 8mm and 16mm films for his local Young Cinema Society chapter and intended to study film. When he applied for university admission in Tehran, however, he was dismayed to find out the school system had instead assigned him to a theater program. But he came to appreciate the effect studying theater had on his writing abilities. Farhadi says he eventually fell in love with the canon of theatrical literature.[4] While completing his bachelor's degree at Tehran University, Farhadi soon found a job at the Islamic Republic of Iran Broadcasting (IRIB) writing radio scripts, and continued to work there while finishing his master's degree in theater direction at Tarbiat Modarres University.[5]

Because of the success of his radio plays, Farhadi was soon offered the chance to write and direct television episodes for well-known television serials, including *Tale of a City*. Before making his debut as a film director,

Farhadi wrote the screenplay for Ebrahim Hatamikia's *Low Heights* (2001), a commercial and critical success in Iran.[6]

The next crucial step for Farhadi was to move into the art form he'd originally loved: cinema. He debuted *Dancing in the Dust* in 2003 and has directed six films over a ten-year span, each work bringing him to new heights of fame and success both domestically and internationally.

This book introduces Farhadi as the new Iranian auteur, whose social realism—observations on the culture at large driven through a documentary-like lens—is skillfully effaced by a highly refined version of the melodrama.

Yet his social commentary—though bleak, sometimes damning—never feels didactic or punishing (one Iranian critic found his screenplays to be "indirectly sociological").[7] Mostly, the ideology remains ambiguous or invisible, buried underneath a myriad of interpretations that are more informative about the viewer than the work itself. Farhadi questions the way things work in today's world, and if there's one thing his films do blame, it's the disastrous but near-invisible effect of modern times on the frazzled Iranian psyche, torn between tradition and modernity.

"What Farhadi is staging, in essence, is psychological interiority, a modernist notion of the subject that insists that we cannot know one another solely from our actions, that only through communication and discourse can we overcome 'separation,' a basic human condition," Michael Sicinski elucidated in his review of *A Separation*.[8]

One key ideology underlining all of Farhadi's works is a refusal to allow absolute values—those driven by religion, mostly, but also by privilege and politics—to continue to drive the discourse in Iranian society. His pluralistic perspective on morality is a refreshing and much-needed creative expression in a film culture that has become creatively eroded from censorship.

Joseph Burke epitomized the filmmaker's sensibilities best: "Each of Farhadi's directed films explicitly concern the pressures of social life and how human interaction develops to pose deeply complex, some say intractable difficulties."[9]

Farhadi's portrayal of this kind of alienation in Iranian society has been correlated to Fyodor Dostoevsky, an understandable comparison given that both lack sympathy for fundamentalism and intellectually deconstruct the complicated social relations between people, morality, classes, technologies, and ideology.

It's not surprising or unusual for an artist belonging to the upper-middle class turn a critical eye inward (in Iranian cinema, masters like Kiarostami had begun that practice years ago), and yet Farhadi's viewpoint remains staunchly and impressively neutral on the consequences and outcomes of moral actions, from people who range from the lowest tier of society to the highest. He's not here to tell us whom to judge or why. Farhadi writes to reveal the moral depravity deeply embedded within all of us—Iranian or not, old or young, rich or poor, male or female.

## Interview

**Tina Hassannia: There have been rumors that your next film will be about Prime Minister Mohammad Mosaddegh.[1] Can you tell me about this project?**

Asghar Farhadi: It's one of my dreams to make a film about him and I will definitely do it one day. But that's a really big production and I want it to be seen really well outside of Iran. It won't be my next film because I need to do some more work before I get to that.

**Would you consider it your passion project?**

It is one of them. I think if I don't get to make another film after doing that one, I wouldn't be very upset. Mosaddegh lived a very interesting life, politically and personally. The political parts are what non-Iranians don't know about, and the personal aspects—which are very interesting—are what Iranians don't know much about either.

**You wanted to study cinema in university but were assigned theater/drama instead. Why did this happen, and was it a frustrating experience?**

I did an entrance exam for cinema, where a panel interviewed me mostly about the stories that I had written. They liked it a lot. By that point, I'd made 5 short films, the first when I was 13. At the time of the exam I was 18 or 19. They were very satisfied and found it surprising that I'd made so many films. I was quite certain I'd gotten in because my rank in the country was eighth. When I got the results back I realized I'd been accepted into the theater program at the University of Tehran. I thought it was a mistake because I hadn't even written the test for that program. It was a terrible day for me. I had the wrong image of theater in my head. There was a place during my teenage years where I used to spend time in the afternoons where in the adjacent building a group of people practiced theater. They were doing monologue rehearsals, always yelling very loudly and they were all heavy smokers. They had long beards and hair and I found them all very unappealing. That image of theater stuck with me and I thought if I went to that program in school I'd have to look like them. After a short while I studied, I wanted to change my program, and because I couldn't, I decided to quit. After a while, I stayed in the program and started reading plays. This opened a new world to me and now I'm very happy that I took this path. It had a profound effect on my writing. The familiarity with the contemporary literature of the world, and even Iranian playwrights, was an amazing experience for me that I never would have had if I had gone to cinema school instead.

**Why do you think you fell in love with writing while studying theater instead of, say, directing? Did you get a chance to study other aspects of theater in your studies, or was your program focused on scriptwriting?**

In university, the first two years are common courses, including acting and directing and writing. After two years, you choose your specialty. I knew from the beginning that I wanted to do writing. From a very young age in childhood I knew I wanted to write. Even today, I think of myself more as a writer than a director. After two years in school, I chose playwriting as my specialty. In Farsi we call it "performative writing." It was a very formative period for me, even though I didn't write much. Because I spent a lot of time reading. In those university years, my main takeaway was learning what is good and what is bad in playwriting. For example, there were works that everyone hailed as masterpieces and before university I would applaud them just to fit in. I never knew why [Sadegh Hedayat's] *The Blind Owl* was a great and important text. After university, I comprehended the reasons why a particular text is great. In those university years, I developed my tastes.

**Who are your favorite playwrights and authors?**

In Iran we actually don't have that many great playwrights. There are two or three names that almost everyone you ask will refer to. The playwrights I really liked were Bahram Beizaei and Manouchehr Radin. They were the greatest then, they're the greatest now, and their names will always be present in the history of Iranian playwriting. At the same time, I became familiar with storytellers who had different takes, and each built a different world for me. For example, Mahmoud Dolatabadi, who hasn't written plays, but his stories helped me a lot. Sadegh Chubak was another example, and more than anyone else Gholam-Hossein Saedi. These writers are the golden peak of our contemporary literature. Of the foreign writers, [Henrik] Ibsen was the biggest influence on me. When I read plays, I wished everything were similar to Ibsen's work, including my own. I think in my own work I became heavily influenced by Ibsen. I was fascinated with the intricacies of [Anton] Chekhov's work, but because of the cold and heavy environment of his stories, I never felt emotionally close to them. I also really liked [Tennessee] Williams and [Eugene] Ionesco. There were others too that everyone enjoys, like [William] Shakespeare. I respect some of these works a lot as historical landmarks, but I never really miss them to the point where I want to re-read them.

**Can you tell me about your thesis on Harold Pinter?**[2]

I love Pinter very much because of the way he uses language. Unfortunately, I suspect I'm missing a lot given that he didn't write in Farsi, but even then and in translations, I feel like among playwrights of his magnitude, he has an exceptional use of language. The main trait of his characters is that they say certain things to avoid saying what's actually in their heart. And for us who grew up in Iranian society, this is very tangible. In our literature, elements like irony and metaphor are used very frequently. In a telephone conversation, a lot of people are afraid to be silent and they constantly chat unless the other person is speaking. This kind of talking is often done to conceal something. In Pinter's work the person who talks most is the one who is trying to express himself the least. For example, in *The Dumb Waiter*, I believe they're called Ben and Gus, they're these two people who receive a letter that orders them to kill someone. They don't know who's sent the order but they go to carry it out. They start speaking with each other about completely irrelevant things and we slowly realize that the letter that has arrived asks one of them to kill the other. In order to avoid exposing this secret, they talk endlessly about unrelated things. This element of Pinter's work, the complexity of human beings, is why I love his work so much. Generally, in plays, Iranian or otherwise, people whine too much. They talk too much, but all this talking hasn't got much reason and philosophy behind it. Pinter's work is different. The work of Samuel Beckett, for example, does interesting things with language as well, but not like Pinter's. Beckett's work examines the philosophical condition of man in the postwar society. For this reason, a lot of people don't like Beckett, but I think he has also used language very well. Even better than Ionesco.

**It's interesting that you connect so much with Pinter because his work has always reminded me of the kind of mind games people play with each other in Iranian culture, and this dynamic is very present in your work. Tell me about the work you did at the Young Iranian Cinema Society.**

I was 13 when I made my first short. It was an 8mm film called *Radio*. Those years, they started an initiative that is still active today, though not with the same quality level. It was called the Young Cinema Society. In every city, even in small rural cities, there was an office with a filmmaking coach and a couple of 8mm cameras and raw stock and young adults would go there to make films. Before the revolution, Kanun[3] used to do that. When I was 13, I went there before taking classes. I just brought a screenplay, without even knowing how a script is supposed to look like. I'd just seen it in books. I had handwritten it with really bad handwriting. I took it there and they accepted it, probably because they were amazed that I was so young and could write a film. They found it really interesting. I made that film and it didn't turn out badly. After that, I made a short 8mm film once every year, and also made one 16mm documentary which was destroyed and lost in the laboratory of the Ministry of Culture and Islamic Guidance. It's a shame, it was the best work I did in those days. It was called *Eyes*. It was about some laborers in factories where used glasses would be melted and from the molten glass they'd reshape new glass containers. This activity would release a chemical gas that damaged their eyesight. The film's question was that, knowing you're going blind, how do you continue working? It was a very bleak film, but it never even got to editing. It was lost in the lab. When I entered theater, I thought I would leave cinema forever. I loved theater so much, I thought it was my calling. And when I started working in radio, they offered me the opportunity to write plays and I accepted. The plays were aired nightly. It really helped me get into a writing groove. Then I was offered a TV job and I accepted it. I think it was about 13-14 years ago when I first found the opportunity to work in cinema. First as a writer, then as a filmmaker. The radio plays were 5-10 episodes each. I would work on them for a month each and write all episodes. A few months later they would be aired as a nightly piece and they had tons of listeners. Writing radio plays is very difficult. I didn't have that experience beforehand but it really helped me. Radio listeners are very different from TV and cinema audiences. They're usually lonely souls. I felt that way then, when I was writing for them. I was writing for people who would turn their radio on at 12 a.m. and listen to my play. They were different people and it was interesting for me to be faced with an audience who can't sleep at night. They have their own world.

**You said it was difficult writing these radio scripts, but did you enjoy it?**

Absolutely. It was difficult at first, because there were incredibly rigorous censorship rules, but when the first few of my works were aired, the station had so many listeners that they became more and more lenient with me. I was at an age where I was full of energy and passion. I didn't know the concept of "difficulty." Every day at 6 a.m. I would wake up to write and would write consistently till 10-11 so I could study the rest of the day.

**Did you do this right after graduation?**

Starting in second or third year, I started writing for the radio. After four years at the University of Tehran, I went to another university for a master's degree in directing, but those three years weren't productive because I was so occupied with writing in radio and television that I never attended classes. I can say that I don't think of that as a real university experience.

**When did you move into television?**

When I was working for radio, because my work found lots of listeners, television came to me. Producers offered to do the same plays on TV. But the problem was that going from theater to television was a downgrade. I had a university professor, Mr. Abbas Javanmard, whom I love. When he heard I had gone into television instead of theater, he stopped talking to me until a couple of years ago. Theater people thought I was selling out. It was difficult for me. My thinking was that I wanted to make something new in television and elevate the medium. At first, my work was like everyone else's. Then I started *Tale of the City*, which for the first time talked about certain taboo subjects. It wasn't impressive technically. We didn't have enough resources for that, but it expanded the limited horizons of television at the time. We talked about AIDS for the first time, for example, on Iranian television. It became very successful and had a massive audience. That was the reason a producer came to me and asked me to work on these types of stories in cinema. I don't really believe that television and cinema are bigger media than theater. I think theater is the most established and prestigious of them, but television and film obviously have larger audiences. I hadn't decided to take this career trajectory, but I was taken away from theater and eventually settled in cinema.

**What was your transition from television to cinema like?**

From theater to radio and television wasn't my personal decision. At first, I actually had a terrible feeling about leaving theater. But from television to cinema I felt great. I was at a point where television had started to bother me. After 2-3 years, the authorities had read my hand and were more careful with my work. I wasn't comfortable working there anymore because of these restrictions. My hands were tied, so I wanted to take that next step.

**How did your first film [*Dancing in the Dust*] happen?**

The difference between my first film and the other ones is that the main idea of the story wasn't mine. I've never done that again. I had a friend who told me about a factory in suburban Tehran where people sell snakes in order for the workers to produce medicine from their venom. I visited the place once and its atmosphere was very strange. I really liked it. So I wrote a story about it. The film's story moved away from that original tale because they didn't give me permission to film in that building. In the factory, one of the harrowing things they did was inject snake venom into horses, which would cause the animal to go into shock and it was an incredibly disturbing scene to behold. It was exactly like being bitten by a snake. The horses would convulse and their bodies would produce an antidote, which was then taken from their blood and used to produce medicine. It was absolutely barbaric. When I saw it, I couldn't believe my eyes. I wanted my story to be about that but they found out and threw me out and never let me back in. So I took my story in the direction of those who find the snakes in the desert. The story was finished in 3-4 months, and with a very small crew the film was made. I think the entire process took about ten months.

**Can you expand on your formative experience of falling in love with cinema? I believe the anecdote was something along the lines of you walking midway into a film, and in your head you tried to recreate its beginning?**

When I saw that film in theaters, I must have been about six years old. I went with my cousin. I forget which film it was. It must have been from the Eastern Block. I say six because it was a foreign film and after the revolution they only showed foreign films in theaters for a couple of years. That film stuck with me because its lead character was a young adult boy who kills the villain in the film. At that age, I sympathized with the boy and he became a kind of a hero for me. So I went back to recreate his experience.

That attempt of recreating the first part of the film is my oldest memory of wanting to write. I had an intense desire to write down my notes, but I didn't know how to write yet. That's why it stuck with me. Later, whenever I watched a film that lingered with me for hours, I wanted the opportunity to make the rest of it. When I watched good films, when they ended, I was bothered. I wanted them to continue, so in my head, I would build the rest of the story and develop those characters further. If you remember—you might be too young—there was a period after the revolution during the [Iran-Iraq] war, when they began to show war films about WWII on television. This was to encourage a sense of bravery and patriotism in people. I remember that on Friday afternoons, we'd always watch a film like this. Friday afternoons are gloomy to begin with, and that grey atmosphere would help me continue the story of the characters in those gloomy films in my head. They never had good endings, because I'd write them in my gloomy Friday afternoon mood. Maybe the fact that everyone now thinks my films are sad started then. I imagine Sunday afternoons there are similarly sad.

**Your stories all start forming when you come across a striking image that lingers in your mind, compelling you to fill in the details. More than once, you've described this thought process as "finding a suit for a button." Is that what happened with the factory for** *Dancing in the Dust***?**

There were two images that were the button for this film's suit. One was the horses injected with venom. But about the urban part of the film: in Tehran, I always used to pass by some place where there was a bridge under which there was a very poor house for immigrants. When I passed on the bridge, I could see everything in their house. It was a naked house. You could see everything, even their bedroom. It was like a naked woman sitting under the bridge. When I wrote the story about the prostitute, I thought her residence could be that house. You see the place in the film actually. I worked in that very house, and it's still there when I pass by.

***Dancing in the Dust* has an interesting conundrum for its protagonist. He loves his wife very much, but is forced to divorce her so that he**

**and his parents aren't socially shamed. What is your view on the culture of marriage in Iran?**

We live in a country that has undertaken big cultural shifts in the past few decades. A few decades ago, the meaning of marriage and its duration had a completely different definition than it does now. Traditional families still define it differently from more modern families. Traditional families didn't consider it a necessity for the man and woman to love each other to get married. In our culture, love stories are not realistic stories. They belong to legend. In real life, if love happened before marriage, it would have been a strange event, worthy of a story. It was negatively looked upon even. People got married and maybe after marriage they'd fall in love or maybe they'd just live together out of habit. In the modern world, the definition of marriage has largely shifted. People fall in love and then decide to live together, by marriage or without it. In Iran, the traditional sector of the society still looks at marriage in the old way. When people get married, their first goal is to ensure theirs is a union that will last before they make it official. Because of this, families feel responsible and involve themselves in the marriage process. They believe marriage is irreversible. Divorce is an abnormal concept. Families try to create a sense of complete security so that the marriage will last, and they don't view love between the partner as a guaranteeing factor. Social status, for example, is a better guarantee. Although it seems like this boy and girl deeply love each other, the boy's family doesn't approve of the girl's mother's job and hence they see no long-term guarantee in a long-term marriage like that.

**Do you believe the taboo subject of prostitution had any impact on the film's poor box office sales?**

Actually, in our country, whatever is taboo finds a massive audience. People love what's banned.

**In that case, in your opinion, what were the problems with *Dancing in the Dust*'s release?**

This was my first film. Its name and its image aren't exactly appealing. And in truth, it isn't a populist film. It only has two characters. It's kind of like theater. It was not unusual for it not to sell. The film only screened in a small number of cinemas with limited advertising. Later, when my other films came out, many people watched *Dancing in the Dust* on DVD. It's the only one of my films that producers have asked to remake in the U.S. In other Asian countries, like Japan, they wanted *A Separation*. In India, too. *The Past* is being reworked as a play in Germany and Finland and it's going on stage next year. In the US, the only film they wanted was *Dancing in the Dust*—possibly because the atmosphere is very similar to westerns. But the idea doesn't appeal to me. Back when it was first released, the critics watched it but the public didn't really respond.

**Would it be interesting for you to see another director remake *Dancing in the Dust* in the US?**

Of course. Every time I write a script, I like to know how another filmmaker would see it. But generally, they change films so much in remakes that in the end, I don't think I would like it.

**You won awards for the film at the Fajr Festival and the Asia-Pacific Film Festival. What was the impact and publicity of those awards?**

Back then, films that won awards would be viewed as artistic films with no audience appeal by people and cinema owners. Films were divided into two categories: those that won awards at festivals and those that were screened in theaters for people. There was no in between. The awards that the film won unfortunately put it on one side of the barrier. After *Fireworks Wednesday* I was able to bridge that gap. Every one of my films has been one of the best-selling of the year and has also won awards. People and critics have both responded to it.

**You are one of the few filmmakers who has been able to do that in Iran, to find a common area between artsy films and populist ones.**

This divide existed before the revolution too. For example, Nosrat Karimi's films were one of the few that could bridge the gap. Both audiences and the intelligentsia responded to it. I've never liked to separate the two. I've wanted to find audiences between people and critics. It's important for me to make that happen today too.

**You've mentioned reading Syd Field in interviews.**[4] **Has he always been an influence for you? Does he translate to the realms of theater and radio?**

Actually, Field gets most of his ideas from classical plays. You can see his ideas at play in really old plays much more than new films. But he's applied them to screenwriting as well. When I was in university, I realized what Field was saying was very close to the structure of the type of plays I really liked. Those are the guidelines I tried to follow. But in my last three films, I've distanced myself from his guidelines, somewhat. But because he gets the foundation of his work from classical plays and I've learned the base of my knowledge from classical plays, there's quite a lot of similarity.

**Even though your latest films feature poor characters, the focus is always on the experience of the middle class. Why did you choose to make this move, and would you consider making films about poor characters again?**

The most important reason that I subconsciously changed my stories about the middle class was due to the fact that I have always belonged to this tier of society. I'm close to these stories personally. The first two films and the plays I wrote were about the lower classes because back then I was more influenced by other Iranian writers like Sadeq Chubak, Bozorg Alavi, Sadegh Hedayat, and Mahmoud Dolatabadi, whose stories dealt with the themes of the lower classes. They were mostly leftist writers, and all their stories were about equality—particularly economic equality. I was very influenced by that. After *Beautiful City*, with *Fireworks Wednesday*, I started becoming more and more influenced by what actually went on in my life. This was the main reason for the shift in my storytelling. Another reason when I thought about that shift later, maybe with *Fireworks* or *About Elly*, is that in the modern world the destiny of a society is determined by its middle class. I wanted to discuss this tier of the society more. The great thing about middle-class stories is that you can at once discuss other rungs of the society. In *Fireworks*, *About Elly*, and *A Separation*, even though my focus is on the middle class, I've found plenty of opportunities to introduce lower-class characters into my stories.

**Starting with *About Elly* and especially with *A Separation* your visual articulations and language became much more refined. Do you believe you have grown as a director with each film?**

A big part of it comes from the unconscious. Any story that comes to my mind brings a visual language with itself. The visual language imposes itself on the filmmaker. But the unconscious mind itself is heavily influenced by what goes on in my daily life, by my conversations with people. It's like the rules of driving. You learn them and then you unconsciously apply them without ever thinking about it as you drive. Those rules are just imprinted on your unconscious. The information is filtered in your brain that way. The visual language I employed in *About Elly* and *A Separation* comes from my unconscious, but is taken from my previous experiences and the stories I encounter in real life. When I make a film, I don't think to myself, *This is the cinematic language I'm going to choose for this film*. I let the visual language come to me just as the story does.

**I'd like to ask you about censorship, but I'm slightly embarrassed since it's the most prevalent subject when journalists interview Iranian filmmakers. I believe one of the reasons there remains so much confusion and curiosity in the West is because the process is so very rarely explained and it all seems so vague. Can you tell me about your experience working with censors and getting scripts approved, and how has it changed over the past decade?**

This is a very long discussion, both about censorship in the world and in Iran specifically. I believe there is a big censorship system in the entire world that takes different shapes in different countries. In Iran, the government implements it and it directly tells you what subjects you can or cannot make films about. In other countries, there are implicit systems. They don't tell you what to make or not, but there are subjects that would provoke attacks, so you prefer to steer away from them altogether. That is, unless you have the same angle on the story as the hegemony in the society. That's also a type of censorship. For example, in the US or Europe, there's freedom and you can supposedly talk about whatever you want, but if you are in the minority and keep talking about something that the society at large doesn't like, the media puts you under so much pressure it forces you to stop discussing it on your own. Take the topic of Israel at the moment, for example. When I talk to my friends about it, they agree with me but when I ask them to write about it in the papers, the ones who live in the US or Europe say they prefer not to do that. In the West, people don't bring up the fact that these implicit types of censorship exist. In Iran, it's governmental. When you want to make a film, you have to go to MCIG (the Ministry of Culture and Islamic Guidance). You submit the script to a team there. The government assigns some of the team members and some are filmmakers. They read the script and tell you whether or not you can make the film. Mostly they give permission with some revisions to the script. Then you get the certificate that allows you to make the film. You complete production and come back to the same ministry with your film in hand. Another team now watches your work and comments on it to see whether it is distributable and fits within the ministry's guidelines. Around the world, people are surprised how so many great films get made in Iran despite the censorship system. But the censorship system here is curious and hard to understand for others. For example, the team that reviews the script is not the same one that watches the film. Some filmmakers submit a script and then make a different film and since the two teams don't collaborate, they're not aware of this. The other point is that we have a very special country. I love this about us, actually. This team is not made up of a bunch of bearded guys with masks on their faces in a dark room, as if they're Taliban. When you submit your script, if they reject it, your assistant can call and discuss it, and then people get in arguments and fights and stop talking to each other for a while, and then somehow they find way to skirt around issues and make their films despite all difficulties. The other thing is that this system does not operate by rules. It's like your city's weather. Rain in the morning, sun at noon, snow in the afternoon. (Laughter.) After a while of living in this country, you get the hang of this. You learn the best times to submit your film, because you find out the night before they've had a good time. If you send your film after they've had a bad night, it won't get it made. After you live in Iran for a while, you learn how to navigate these things. I make jokes, but it doesn't mean that this is easy. Films are tough to get made, and censorship over a long period of time is detrimental to the quality of films. When censorship is nascent, filmmakers try to find new ways to make their projects. They even find a new filmic language. But in the long run, it kills creativity. That's why Iranian cinema was very successful a while ago because it was fresh for the whole world, but now creativity is mostly gone. There is no new language. What they could do to overcome the obstacle of censorship has already been done and finding new methods is very difficult.

**A professor of mine once described how societies shift from conservative to liberal views and back again, and compared it to a pendulum. I like this analogy because it means that if society is always shifting, we will soon have another period in Iran in which affairs become relaxed and more films can be made.**

That's correct. In effect, I can't give a general and consistent definition about the social condition in Iran. The pendulum analogy makes you understand how difficult the conditions of filmmaking in Iran are. But at the same time, that's what makes it interesting for me. Tolerating a constant, monotonic situation is difficult for me. It's a challenge that I welcome. When I finish my film, I feel a sense of victory that I think is better than the feeling of someone who makes films in, say, Germany. I've overcome tougher obstacles. In Iran, filmmaking is much cheaper than it is in the US and Europe. There, it's difficult to obtain financing. That makes filmmakers very tired. Here you need much less money. You can make a very good one with $400k. In the US, that amount of money is a joke, unless you make a tiny independent film. Here, we don't have that financial problem, but we have censorship and other problems to make up for that.

**There was a Tabnak report that posited the financial death of Iranian cinema is mostly because of the high salary of Iranian stars. Is this situation prevalent, and is the number of producers dwindling?[5]**

Many films are made in Iran today despite their cheapness. And, by the way, this is cheap compared to other countries, but not compared to Iranian standards. But because fewer people are going to cinemas in Iran, these films don't make money. There are fewer cinemas in Iran today than the time of the revolution, even though the population has multiplied. That's why most films can't make their own production costs back, unless the government pitches in. Which is why the Iranian film industry is dependent on the government, and this in turn makes censorship even stronger—unless you make very small films that don't need financial assistance. The number of films in which stars demand massive salaries is actually not very high. The stars who demand such salaries aren't many, either. They assume that the film sells because of their name, which is only natural. There's no discussion to be had about it. But in our country, the social act of going to the cinema to see movies, like in many other places worldwide, is becoming obsolete. People prefer to sit in an enclosed environment and watch films on their television. Additionally, there are so many satellite and television and home-video options, people don't like to go to the movies anymore. Generally, our people shy away from gathering together in public these days. Instead of going to a public pool, people prefer to have a private pool in their backyard. Instead of going to the park, they like to have a private garden. They like to be far from each other. Have you ever seen how Iranians outside of Iran socialize with each other? They try to avoid each other. We are one of the few cultures who act that way. Moviegoing is a public exercise, but in our modern Iran, people don't feel comfortable doing that and the cinema is suffering financially because of that more than ever before.

**Glass is such an important visual motif in your films. You mentioned in an interview[6] that this began with *Fireworks Wednesday*, but I think it goes back much earlier to your first film. The symbolism behind the use of glass, however, is always changing in your films, even within the same film. Sometimes it's a barrier preventing two people from communicating; other times it's broken from an emotional reaction and signifies some kind of existential or moral breakdown. Why is this?**

In *Dancing in the Dust*, and in *Beautiful City*, these details are symbolic. When you see them, such as the ring in the water in *Dancing in the Dust*, you think that there is a meaning behind that. But as my films progressed, I realized that I have to turn these elements from symbols into signs. The difference is that when you see a symbol, you're immediately aware that a filmmaker has put it there for you to read a meaning behind it. Signs are something where its significance escapes you on the first viewing. But with repetition and in the context of the film, they instill a sense of meaning for you. For example, in *The Past*, when you see the two main characters on either side of the glass in the beginning, and they can't hear each other, it doesn't mean anything to you. But when that motif is repeated throughout the film, you realize that windows and glass and doors are signs that point you to an emotion. They don't mean anything individually. The same goes for the windows in *A Separation*. In *About Elly, Fireworks Wednesday, A Separation*, and *The Past*, these signs are very similar to mundane elements of daily life. When you see them, they don't occupy your mind as anything meaningful. In *Dancing in the Dust* and *Beautiful City*, it's different. The minute you see any of these objects, you realize that there is something deeper beneath the image. You're distracted. I didn't like that, so I gradually changed my language.

**In an interview you explained how you were influenced to write *Beautiful City* because of the poverty-stricken pockets of society you saw while commuting to school.[7] What did you see, and what kind of stories did you hear?**

The film's story wasn't entirely inspired by that location. I already had a story in mind. But for its location, I was looking around and I happened to find it as I was travelling between Tehran and Isfahan on the train. I saw this neighborhood, mostly occupied by immigrants. It was very poor and the train track pierced through the middle of the neighborhood. The houses were incredibly close to it and the constant movement of the train in the area had made the population very aggressive and unsettled. That worked very well for me, but when you stayed there awhile, you find a humane aspect in their lives. That's why I chose this neighborhood. I generally love trains in the movies. I incorporated them again in *The Past*. The fact that this train constantly moved through their lives, even when they were singing lullabies to their kids, was appealing to me. Trains have a nostalgic and romantic feel to them.

**I read that when you shot *Beautiful City* you were more relaxed with the script, whereas with *Dancing in the Dust* you followed your script to a tee. What were the reasons for this? My guess is that you were still new to directing when you made *Dancing in the Dust*.**

It's been many years. I can't remember correctly how much difference there was between the script and the final film. There were instances of scenes that weren't originally in the script that [were] just shot on set. There's one scene, for example, in the neighborhood we discussed, where there is a mother singing a lullaby to her child and at the same time a very loud train is passing through. I was wondering how the child could fall asleep. I turned that into a scene where Firoozeh sings to her child on the rooftop as the train passes. I didn't do this sort of thing as much in *Dancing in the Dust*. I mostly went by script. But in *Beautiful City* I did move with more freedom. Actors had some input too. For example, the girl who plays the disabled girl in the film, Gharibian's daughter, wasn't in the script in that shape, but her character developed during filming. For example, the scene where she tells a story for Firoozeh's young child was not originally in the script, but was discovered on set.

**Has this process continued in your future films?**

In *The Past*, I worked exactly what was in the script, because I don't speak French and I didn't have the chance to change things around and improvise. In *About Elly*, I left the environment more open, but in *A Separation* I worked [with] exactly what was in the script. It depends a lot on the actors and the atmosphere behind the scenes. It's not always the same.

**You have a very interesting rehearsal process. For *A Separation*, your cast didn't get to rehearse the script that intensely, but you spent months doing character development, having them rehearse scenes that weren't in the movie, and so on.[8] It reminded me of Mike Leigh and theater exercises in general.**

I've talked to Mike Leigh about this and we compared our processes. Mike doesn't have a script. He brings in the actors he likes, works with them for 7-8 months and, during that rehearsal process, writes the script. He starts with an idea and develops the script over a few months of exercise. I have a fully written script. I bring in the actors after, but I don't like to hand them the script and ask them to play it, because they don't have ownership of their roles yet. They feel like it's all the author's work. In rehearsals, I spend time developing these characters and their story lines. But we rewind back to point zero. I ask the actors to walk the same path with me so they feel like they're building the characters themselves. In those rehearsals, the actors gain ownership of the roles. They feel a sense of pride and creation about their role. That's why in my films, you see the characters defending themselves very often, because in rehearsal they've grown to think of the characters as pieces of themselves. In rehearsal, we don't really play out the script. We just practice different scenes, so the actors remove their distance with the role.

**For almost every story of yours, I've come across its origins and how the ideas were planted in your head. Except for one: Where did the initial idea for *About Elly* come from?**

From a few different places. Foremost, when I was a student in university, I had a few very close friends with whom I would go on a lot of trips, mostly to Shomal [Caspian seaside]. Just a bunch of young boys and girls. These trips became nostalgic treasures for me in retrospect. I always wanted to make a film about trips to the North for Iranian youngsters. That was one trigger for the story. Another was an image in my head of a man at dusk on a slightly cold night who stands by the sea with wet clothes, looking as if he were searching for something earlier in the water. This was an image that made me think he might have been looking for the body of his wife, who might have drowned. So the story basically came together based on these two separate images. Like with *A Separation*—a film that was ignited because of my image of a man washing his dad in the shower—this was directly imported into the film.

**You've been making films for a decade now. What did you learn from each film, especially between *Fireworks Wednesday* and *About Elly*?**

I learned many new things, some that I'm probably unaware of. But the main thing is that details became more important for me. Mundane, daily events became more important. I focus more on details now. Small things that probably aren't important to us in real life. Another thing I realized after *Fireworks Wednesday* was that audiences are incredibly intelligent, and there is no need to repeat anything or say it loudly. When you talk quietly as a director, the audience pays more attention to your film. When you talk loudly, it will actually distract the audience from the details in your film. That means I didn't want to show off themes. I hid the themes under the film's story. This reached its peak in *The Past*. Had I made that film after *Beautiful City*, I would have explained many more details about the past life of each character, but now I don't. I believe that's the audience's job to open the film up. These are the two big truths that I came to at that stage. And another thing that's important is that anybody in any situation has a reason for everything they do, and as a filmmaker, I have no right to stand on a character's side and judge the rest from that point of view.

**Your characters always have a reason for what they do—this is a very important characteristic in your work. You don't really write bad characters. But the druggie husband in *Beautiful City* is a bit of an exception.**

*Beautiful City* was my second film, but even in that character of the druggie father, when we first meet him we don't feel good about him, mostly because of his appearance. But there's a scene where he enters a room and hugs a child who is crying and there we sympathize with him. We understand him and don't blame him at that stage. I don't remember ever having characters in my films that are completely negative or to be blamed for the bad elements in the film. In *Beautiful City*, there are two characters like that. One is the druggie husband, the other is the second wife of [Faramarz] Gharibian. These two characters are kind of lonely, segregated characters. The audience empathizes with them, even though we might not be able to put ourselves in their shoes.

**Actually, there's a third character who can be described this way, too: the warden at the beginning of the film. He's like a contrast to the other warden character.**

Yes, there are two characters, a tall man and a bald one. You're talking about the bald one. If I were to make the film now, I wouldn't make that character as he is. He was too negative because of his violence and aggression and he was very typical of what cinema shows you of prison wardens. If I were to make the film now, I would turn him into a real character. But even in that film, he has one sentence that turns him from being an archetype into being a real character. He's aggressive, he's violent towards kids, he's nihilistic and doesn't think anything will come out of the kid's efforts. But eventually when the friend is about to go to the man's house to get their permission, the warden tells him not to go empty-handed. And that changes our perspective of that man's character. That gesture means a lot in Iranian culture; to not go to a place empty-handed shows kindness and humanity. When I say I don't have negative characters, it doesn't mean that they all do good things. They make a lot of mistakes, but somehow in some place they show something of themselves that proves to us that they are human too and have emotions and justifications.

**Another development with your later films is how bigger they became in terms of production scale, particularly the differences between *About Elly* and *A Separation*, and between *A Separation* and *The Past*.**

Between *A Separation* and *The Past*, you're right. The scale of production changed immensely. *The Past* had everything—resources and budget galore. But between *About Elly* and *A Separation* the production budget and scale didn't change at all. They were exactly the same, actually. *The Past* happens in Europe, so obviously the location and the actors were much more expensive and filming took longer than expected. But when I make films, I don't like to make them expensive at all.

**Was there more pressure for you as a filmmaker when you were creating *The Past*? Did having a larger budget change anything?**

No. It doesn't make any difference for me what the budget is. I mean there's a difference, obviously, but I don't feel any more responsibility. I always feel maximum responsibility when I make films anyway. It could be as cheap as *Beautiful City* or as expensive as *The Past*. I was no more relaxed when I was making *Beautiful City*. I always feel the same during shooting, actually.

**It must have been strange for you to make a film in France, given how production rules differ from country to country. What was it like working within different parameters?**

Filmmaking in Europe is closer to filmmaking in Iran than the system in America. In the US, for everything there's ten people doing an assigned job.

In Iran, everybody does many things, which I like a lot more. In Europe, everyone had their own massive trailer. Mine was so big and had everything I could need, but I feel like these kinds of resources have no bearing on the quality of the film. I think these are extra costs. In Iran, without these, we make films. Although I'm not advocating the Iranian system where nothing you need is available. But a middle ground between the difficulty of Iran and the ease of France is ideal.

**Speaking of the crew you had with *The Past*: this was the first film you made without Hayedeh Safiyari. In my opinion, she really understands your storytelling and it shows in the finished product. She's such an amazing editor. I really missed her presence in this film.**

I agree with you completely. In *The Past*, because Ms. Safiyari wasn't there, I felt like I was missing something. She didn't speak French, but I needed someone who spoke the language, so if I had 10 takes of a scene, the editor could tell me where the dialogue has come out best. Because she didn't speak French, I had to work with a French editor [Juliette Welfling] who had a great resume. But she didn't understand the language of my films. She had seen them, but it was hard for me and took a long while to explain what I wanted exactly. If Hayedeh spoke French, I would have been a lot more comfortable. I think she's one of the best editors in the world.

**(Laughter.) A week ago [my translator] Amir said the exact same thing!**

I really hope for my next film, even though it's not in Farsi, that I can again have Hayedeh on my team.

**Though you've said that you don't let awards interfere with his work. I'm assuming you try to do the same thing with audience reception. Obviously, after *A Separation*, your success exploded internationally and I have to say, no matter how hard one might try not to feel an influence, at some point it must make a difference. Do you think even in some small way, reception affects you?**

Of course. It has an impact. But what really happened was that before *A Sep-*

*aration* became popular and played festivals or received such a reception by the French public (one million tickets sold) or the American public, which could have put me under a lot of pressure, I had already devised *The Past* and the film was in pre-production before *A Separation* was even screened to the public. I was already making *The Past* and that meant that mentally I didn't have the capacity to deal with the events surrounding *A Separation* and its popularity as such. When I was in the US for the Oscars, I kept making calls and sending emails from my hotel room trying to work out the pre-production details of *The Past*. But of course, massive reception influences your work, unfortunately. There's a sensation in you that makes you want to try to impress the same audience and cater to them, which can become dangerous and detrimental.

**What was it like for you growing up as an aspiring filmmaker? Did your parents encourage you to study the arts?**

I was very lucky that no one in my family put any pressure on me when I decided to study theater. Because as you know, I had started making films when I was 13, so when I got to university age, they had already accepted that I would go that route. My short films were already quite successful. They didn't particularly encourage me, but there was no attempt to stop me, either. I was free to study what I wanted and no one bothered me about it. It wasn't that they didn't care, but luckily there was a relatively liberal atmosphere in my family.

**Are there any other artistic people in your family?**

Not really, but my younger brother also writes scripts for television and he also studied theater.

**Every film of yours deals with relationships and marriage. It's a very important dynamic in your stories, and many of the conflicts turn on the obligations characters have as wedded or to-be-wed partners. Do you think you have some kind of fascination with marriage, or is it simply that relationships make for great dramatic fodder?**

The reason I spend so much time working with the subject of marriage is that I love making films about relationships between people, and family is a very rich source of relationships between people. In a family, you have women, men, old people, young people, kids, everyone. It's a vast ocean. When you write about family, you write about marriage, you write about a couple, which is the oldest relationship between humankind. But even though it is the oldest type of relationship in the world, its problems are always fresh. Like, any man and woman who get married, they throw out all the experiences of other couples in history and they start the counter from zero again. No relationship in history has concerned people as much in history and that's why I like the topic so much. It's a very good tool that allows me to talk about deeper things about people. It's not just about marriage and man and woman. It's an excuse to talk about everything else regarding people.

**Do you think international reception for your films is similar to audience responses at home?**

It's the same inside and out of Iran, really. For example, *A Separation* and *The Past* connected with both the regular people and the critics in Iran. And the same happened in the US, Europe and Japan. One of the things that makes me happy looking back is that I didn't make films that would only appeal to a certain circle. Like the average joe versus the critic, or Iranian versus non-Iranian. But why does that happen? I think if a filmmaker tells a story properly, it will connect with everybody. It makes no difference whether that audience knows cinema or not, whether they go to the cinema for entertainment or something deeper. Separating intelligentsia from the rest of the audience is not acceptable to me. The emotions of people all around the world is the same. When you make a film about human feelings, everyone understands it. What is different is the way people show their emotions in different cultures, but the basic fact of feeling things like love and hate is the same everywhere in the world. An Iranian and a Japanese and a European may express their emotions differently, but it's the same feeling.

**One comment that pops up frequently among non-Iranian critics is how your work is different from other Iranian films, in that they don't conform to their expectation of slow, arthouse cinema.**

True, but that's not only true of Iran. The same goes with countries like Romania and Mexico. There are clichés about arthouse and experimental films from all around the world that they are slow, not entertaining and devoid of drama. This cliché is incorrect and can be broken. I think with a few of my films, I've been able to break that image of Iranian cinema. We have many good films in Iran that have a fast rhythm, but these films are not generally exhibited outside of Iran.

**The Fajr Festival premieres all the major Iranian films for the public, and it effectively decides their destinies all at once in a span of one week. Do you think this is harmful for Iranian cinema?**

I understand that. It's a problem with the Fajr Festival. And it has many other issues, too. It's one of the most political festivals in the world. If you look at the names of its different strands, you'll see how politically loaded they are. And as you said, they screen all films at once, which isn't good. But I still love the festival! We live in a country where there are no events that can create public euphoria and bring a lot of people together. For example, we don't have music festivals or dance festivals or food festivals. This is our one and only, but with all its troubles and issues, it entertains thousands of young people for 10 days and creates excitement. So I want it to stay as is. What else would young Iranians be excited about in the winter? You look around the world and there are celebrations and carnivals. We don't have celebrations in Iran. We look down on happiness in some ways! But look at what happens at the festival: all the excitement, people talking behind each other's backs, people booing films, all the stories and arguments. This creates so much excitement and I think it's necessary for our society.

## Dancing in the Dust

*Shattered Glass*

*Nazar is happily married to his new wife, Rayhaneh, but is forced to divorce her after his parents hear rumors about Rayhaneh's mother, an alleged prostitute. While Nazar works double shifts at his factory job in order to pay off two sets of loans—his divorce fee on top of a marriage loan he owes Rayhaneh—creditors show up looking to take him to prison. His friend and colleague, Amri, sneaks him into the back of a van belonging to a snake hunter. When the vehicle's owner, a near-silent old man, finds out a tramp has been following him into the desert, he refuses to accept Nazar's apology and even tries to hurt him. The two oscillate between quarrelling and ignoring each other out in the desert, revealing the depths of their loneliness (the ever-nosy Nazar, for example, finds a picture of the man's ex-wife). But finally they form a strange male bond when a snake bites Nazar and the Old Man is forced to amputate Nazar's finger in order to save his life. Driving to the hospital, the Old Man opens up to Nazar, admitting he killed the adulterer who slept with his wife. While registering the unconscious Nazar at the hospital, the administration forces him to pay for Nazar's surgery. He sells his van and belongings in order to help Nazar and drops off the money on his bed. Nazar*

*impulsively disappears with the cash, leaving the Old Man in a bind. Nazar uses the money to pay off his debts. When Nazar later goes to look for the Old Man, he can only find the remainder of his belongings—everything is there, except for the photo of the Old Man's wife.*

---

*Raghs dar Ghobar* (*Dancing in the Dust*) begins Asghar Farhadi's cinema with a shot that will become his signature visual motif: glass. The film's first image is of a hand wiping condensation off a car window, providing a passing glimpse of a statue of Garshasp, a character from Ferdowsi's epic poem *Shahnameh*. It's a brutish monument of a king slaying a dragon connoting Iranian masculinity, mythical heroism, and the need to control nature. This idea is underscored by a ceremonial-like drumming that begins the film—*zurkaneh* music, consisting of traditional percussion instruments and poetry performed in Iranian gymnasiums, a physical and metaphorical arena dominated by men.

Symbolically, the image of Garshasp is fitting, given some of the ideas present in *Dancing in the Dust*. Nazar (Yousef Khodaparast) is a young, foolish Turkish boy who must prove himself as a man to every character in the film. First are his parents, who demand he divorce his wife Rayhaneh (Baran Kosari) after causing their family much social disgrace. When the distraught Nazar tries to open up to his best friend and colleague Amri (Jalal Sarhad Seraj), he refuses to sympathize with Nazar's situation. Then there's Rayhaneh and her mother, who remain unconvinced of Nazar's ability to pay back his marriage loan. His boss wants to fire him for skipping work, and when Nazar is finally stuck out in the desert with an Old Man (Faramarz Gharibian) who seemingly doesn't care if he dies, Nazar tries his best to impress him and learn how to be useful—become a skillful snake hunter, a bread winner who can provide for his ex-wife, someone who can overcome his circumstances, even if he's been cast out to the desert. Mastery over nature—in this case, a deadly animal—is Nazar's last resort, his last real test of manhood.

*Dancing in the Dust* was not Farhadi's original creation; he collaborated on the story with Alireza Bazrafshan and Mohammad Reza Fazeli. Farhadi describes the film's structure as a hybrid of two different stories. "The desert part of it, which was inspired by westerns, had no relation to anything in my real life," explained Farhadi in an interview. "What sets *Dancing in the Dust* apart from my other films is that it's rooted in cinema itself." While writing, Farhadi discovered he did have a connection with the urban-set parts of the film, particularly the socially prescribed moral dilemma facing the young couple, and the implications of their society which unfairly burdens women like Rayhaneh and her mother. *Dancing in the Dust* was thus a learning exercise for Farhadi—from then on, he only made films that inspired a strong personal connection.[1]

Despite Farhadi's domestic name recognition, the film wasn't a success, due to the production's lack of marketing and the fact that it only screened in three theaters in Iran. But this did little to dissuade Farhadi and he even funded his next film (*Beautiful City*) with the same producer.[2]

Though Farhadi says the film has garnered its fans throughout the years, he's not inclined to re-watch the film anytime soon.[3] If he's a little embarrassed about his first effort, it's understandable but unfair, because *Dancing in the Dust* has more than its fair share of charms. And it's a fascinating work insofar as it reveals the beginnings of his style and predilections. The film touches on some of the more problematic aspects of marriage in Iran—the interpretation of its usefulness in Islam and the ways in which women are devalued—in a way that underscores a bittersweet reality for its characters who are unwitting victims to institutionalized prejudice.

*Dancing in the Dust* also reveals Farhadi's burgeoning gift for elliptical storytelling. The opening sequences—which intersperse intertitles with short, animated snapshots of narrative—establish the doomed love between Nazar and Rayhaneh and the impulsiveness with which the young man took out a marriage loan, believing in the longevity of their love.

One of these short scenes shows the jovial couple looking at a tarot card reading (using regular playing cards). Nazar melodramatically insists that the two of them are far apart, noting the several cards between the queen (Rayhaneh) and jack (Nazar). Notably, one of the cards separating the two, adjacent to the jack, is the king of spades, which foreshadows the Old Man whom Nazar encounters later in the film.

Rayhaneh, a non-believer in fortune telling, tells Nazar to read the cards in whatever way that will promise them a happy future. But Nazar, whose knack for petulant histrionics is one of the film's greatest sources of humor (or displeasure, depending on your tolerance for his antics), idealizes their love differently. He is compelled to repeatedly test Rayhaneh on the durability of their relationship. In the final vignette of the credits sequence, he watches a Bollywood film in which the heroine must walk on broken glass in order to save her lover. "Would you do that for me?" he asks Rayhaneh seriously. She responds glibly but pragmatically: yes, but only with shoes on! The two laugh. Nazar is both upset by this answer and amused, so he throws his apple at her, causing the window behind her to break.

Throughout this short and sweet credit sequence, Farhadi alternates between visual and aural cues to progress the story as it switches back and forth between vignettes and credit titles. For example, instead of plainly showing their wedding, the film focuses on the one salient aspect about their marriage: money. An offscreen store clerk asks Nazar if he has a guarantor for his loan as he presses his government IDs on the table.[4] Nazar exuberantly nods his head yes, though the bitter truth is that he won't be able to pay it off. This brief scene is introduced by the sound of female ululation—the kind of clamor strongly associated with Persian weddings—to communicate that the wedding has happened.

Once this montage reaches its conclusion—after Nazar asks Rayhaneh to walk on broken glass for him—an undeniable, sad reality sets in upon the following scene: Nazar's parents are forcing him to divorce Rayhaneh due to the allegations about her mother. They also guilt him for disgracing their family. Nazar, in denial about the matter, demands irrational requests from his parents and Rayhaneh. He suggests to her that they can remain together only under one condition: if she simply never talks to her mother again. He is also confounded by his religious faith, which deems him a sinner either way. He's bad for having married the daughter of a prostitute, and he's damnable for divorcing her. He rashly questions his mother's religious logic even though it's useless. At least Nazar can whine to his mother, who still accepts him. His father simply gives him the cold shoulder.

One of the most crucial revelations at the end of the film is that Nazar had known all along about the rumors. In a moment of doleful confession with the Old Man, Nazar admits that he'd heard about the mother and married Rayhaneh anyway, hoping that their love would be enough. It's a tragic moment that explains a lot of the doomsday talk Nazar facetiously employs in the film's opening scenes, and it reveals not only his foolishness but also a deep masochistic desire to find love in all the wrong places.

Before Nazar is forced to escape from authorities, he and Rayhaneh finalize their divorce in court. Their dynamic does not resemble that of an unhappily married couple. Indeed, their childish whispers to each other remind the viewer that they are still very much in love, yet they must shift between their public and private identities in front of the judge. They lie about no longer loving each and agreeing to separate on civil terms, and this wooden performance undermines the entire social and legal structure of marriage. The film recalls a key scene in *Divorce Iranian Style* (1998) in which one of the subjects brazenly lies to a judge about her husband's disgraceful behavior, sharing a wink with the camera. In a society where civil liberties are regularly stripped away, Iranians frequently and understandably resort to deception to achieve their goals, deftly manipulating the loopholes of a draconian legal system. The decorum Nazar and Rayhaneh follow to finalize their divorce feels more like a performance than a real legal settlement, and it also has very little to do with their love for each other.

Though *Dancing in the Dust* is about Iranian masculinity, its gender politics implicate Rayhaneh and her mother despite the brevity of their appearances. Nazar's fiancé is a simple girl, whose prudence only seems apparent because of her proximity to the fatuous Nazar. She is also young, naive, and unaware of what to do with her life. The subject of her mother is a sensitive one for Rayhaneh, but she is unable to confirm or deny anything when Nazar mentions them. Her dialogue and facial expressions do not sufficiently flesh out her emotional response to the divorce. Her professed willingness is almost an admission of guilt, but other than a few dirty stares and awkward silences, her reticence does little to fully evince this idea or substantiate the mystery.

Rayhaneh's mother appears in one memorable scene. Nazar visits their house, a roaming dilapidated building without any roof that is visible from atop a highway overpass. The interiors can be clearly seen from this level—a fact the film establishes early on, when Nazar first meets Rayhaneh departing a bus on her way home. The film contrasts the building's sheer visibility with numerous clotheslines in the mother's backyard that hide her from view. Nazar appears at a distance from a high level, on the other side of a fence adjacent to her property. His only view is of bundles of garments being draped up one by one. He speaks to an invisible woman whose voice is nonetheless iron-willed. The mother is suspicious of Nazar, believing he only wants to divorce Rayhaneh to get out of paying her marriage portion. Though we hear a headstrong woman, she remains hidden behind a chador and dozens of garment drapes (the effect is at once absurd and astute).

Visually, the setup of this scene symbolizes the double-edged sword faced by Iranian women, especially those of lower classes whose desperation sometimes leads them to prostitution. The house is not naked on purpose—it's just unfortunately situated below a highway, which symbolizes the undeniable force of modernity. The house doesn't beg one to look at it, but it's there nonetheless, almost silently asking you to have the decency to give it privacy, as if it were some kind of architectural concubine. The heavy drapery that prevents Nazar and the viewer from seeing Rayhaneh's outspoken mother speaks to the fact that her culture is contradictory in its demands of women who are expected to honor themselves and still survive. Resorting to something as morally reprehensible as prostitution (the common view in Iranian culture) is not an option, even if it means the only other route is death from starvation. The drapes that shield Rayhaneh's mother also signify the mystery of her alleged profession, and whether or not she actually is a prostitute. The point of the film is not to deny or confirm this fact, but to cast doubt on the certainty of hearsay and its potential to shame people and ruin lives.

*Dancing in the Dust* contains several visually striking images that relay thematic importance. Returning to the subject of Nazar and Rayhaneh's young love and naiveté, there is a notable moment in one of the early, urban-set scenes in which Nazar returns to his workplace, a factory that creates a venom antidote. He walks by several windows with semi-opaque plastic sheets, watching employees controlling a horse that has just been injected with snake venom. A teacher leading his class on a field trip explains that the horse will produce antitoxins in its body that can then be extracted for medicine (intended for humans).

The horse begins to react physically to the injection, thrashing about. "The horse is in shock," the teacher explains to the kids. The factory workers splash the animal with water in order to help it calm down.

The horse, of course, is Nazar. The social pressure to divorce the love of his life has shocked him into the reality of adulthood, but at this early stage in the film (prior to his divorce) he's not yet ready to give up Rayhaneh. After he returns from court, dejected and heartbroken, Amri playfully sprays him with water. Though the symbolism is a little heavy-handed, the idea would have likely worked more fluently had the scene of Amri splashing Nazar been omitted.

Yet to suggest that Nazar has matured overnight as a result of his separation is definitely an exaggeration. The young man still believes he can pay off his creditors—who are at this point looking to jail him—and works double shifts at the factory to both double his salary and avoid the authorities. At work, he comes across a group of snake hunters employed by the factory to bring in the dangerous creatures. Old men stand in circles and smoke. The camera follows them to multiple rows of jars of snakes sitting by a window. Nazar suddenly has a bright idea: if the hunters make good money, maybe he should become one too, to ameliorate his debts while steering clear of the authorities. The world of snake hunting, as portrayed in this film, is a hard and tough business. For an Islamic country like Iran, that means only men can do it. Thus, Nazar's ambition to become a snake hunter ties back to his subconscious desire to prove his masculinity.

Amri, who never passes an opportunity to emasculate his friend, scoffs at the idea. "Pssht! You can't do it," he dismissively tells Nazar as he swaggers in the employee locker room. "That one time I took you to the snake room you were so afraid you almost pissed your pants. And now you want to hunt them?"

Though Amri frequently comes off as a tough and insensitive friend—persistently making callous jokes about Rayhaneh's mother—he does end up saving Nazar from the creditors, who have become wise to Nazar's disappearance. Yet another moral dilemma presents itself here: should Nazar go to jail and serve his time, or escape and try to come up with the money? Amri rationalizes that in jail, Nazar can't work to pay back the loans. In the blink of an eye, Amri comes up with a solution and the desperate Nazar agrees. Suddenly, he's hiding in the back of one of the snake hunter's vans.

The next day, Nazar arrives in the desert and tries to befriend the driver—an old man whose watery eyes hint at lifelong sorrow—but the man has no patience, immediately threatening to hurt him. For the next hour, the film devotes itself to the dynamic between these two characters. One is silent and stoic, lonely and on the verge of death. The other is garrulous, petulant and tries so hard to prove himself he endangers his own life.

One might imagine that this phase of the film to be arduous and boring, and certainly, in some stretches, the pacing does amplify the film's desolate silence to the point of lethargy. Yet considering that the desert section makes up for two-thirds of the film's running time, this is perhaps unsurprising.

We slowly find out about this Old Man—whose sour, silent countenance does little to advise us about his tragic life—as Nazar tries to manipulate his friendship. Gharibian's performance is key to our slow but assured sympathy for this character (it also helps that Nazar is so irritating in contrast, making us feel bad that the Old Man is stuck with him in the middle of nowhere). He is a drug addict. Jars of opium balls attest to this dirty habit, as does one uncomfortable scene in which Nazar hears the Old Man painfully throwing up. The next day, when Nazar cleans the van as a gesture of kindness, his inquisitive nature gets to the best of him. Finding an old, faded photo of a young woman, he can't help but ask who she is. No answer from the Old Man. Farhadi asks us to fill in the blanks: was she his wife? Maybe she passed away.

The Old Man proves to be more of a "man" than Nazar—not by acting tough or superior, but through his later acts of selflessness when Nazar's life is on the line. He begins to open up to Nazar when the young man imperils his life upon being bitten by a snake, causing the Old Man to take some drastic measures. In order for Nazar not to die within several minutes, the Old Man must amputate his finger and rush him to the hospital.

During the drive, pacifying the pain-ridden, fingerless Nazar, the Old Man distracts this younger version of himself by asking about Rayhaneh, trying to understand why Nazar would remain so devout to her after their divorce. "Does she know you're out here?" he questions Nazar. "No. I'd hope she marries a good man, someone better than me," is Nazar's honest and sad reply.

But the Old Man, being an old man, knows better. "If she married someone else, then you'll understand whom you've sacrificed your life for." Little by little, the film carves out the character of the Old Man as someone who has been hurt by love and life.

At first the Old Man is resistant to questions about his life, but eventually reveals that he strangled a man who had been having an affair with his wife. Technically, he's a fugitive, making enough money from snake hunting to get by. He lives in the desert to avoid the authorities and because the silence helps him forget the love of his life. So, too, the opium.

In Farhadi's later films, factual details about characters' shattered dreams would likely be expunged for an abundance of miniscule details that should speak volumes about their disposition. But the men's confessions in *Dancing in the Dust* remain mostly effective pieces of character development.

The ultimate moral dilemma arrives when the Old Man—pressured to register Nazar and pay for his operation at the hospital—must sell his van and belongings in order to produce the money. He does it without missing a heartbeat. Yet his self-sacrifice comes with tragedy. Upon waking up to see the money by his table, a fixed-up Nazar immediately absconds from the hospital. He's never seen that much money before, and it can pay off his marriage loan.

It's an impulsive and morally reprehensible move, but it's also understandable given how poor he is. Yet the consequences this plays on the Old Man are never explained, marking yet another one of Farhadi's films to end on an ambiguous note. While searching for the Old Man, Nazar comes across the van's new owner. Searching through the Old Man's belongings, Nazar finds the box that stashed the old photo of the wife. It's missing.

*Dancing in the Dust* reveals the totality of sacrifice for love. For someone who hated Nazar, the Old Man risked everything he had just so Nazar could live and so, for all we know, the Old Man might already be dead. Nazar has one final meeting with Rayhaneh in order to pay her off. He somberly tells her to study and find a good job. His demeanor suggests that he won't forget Rayhaneh anytime soon, but the film also leaves this question open-ended. He might overcome the calamity, given his youth—or perhaps he'll love her secretly forever. Just like the Old Man, he's destined to keep dancing in the dust.

# *Beautiful City*

*Do the Right Thing*

> To err is human; to forgive, divine. -Alexander Pope
>
> The repayment of a bad action is one equivalent to it. But if someone pardons and puts things right, his reward is with Allah. Certainly He does not love wrongdoers. (Quran: Surat Ash-Shura, 40)

*Boys at a juvenile delinquency center hold a celebration of prisoner Akbar's eighteenth birthday, organized by his friend and fellow prison-mate Ala. But Akbar is in no mood to celebrate his status as a legal adult given that he can now be executed for his crime (at age 16, he killed his girlfriend, Maliheh). The center's counselor breaks up the resultant fistfight and tasks Ala to obtain clemency from Maliheh's father, Mr. Abolqasem, believing the young man has a better chance. Ala is given furlough from his near-finished sentence to make this happen and collaborates with Akbar's sister, Firoozeh. The young woman lives in a desolate part of town with her baby and drug-addicted husband, and has been begging Mr. Abolqasem, a religious man and a doctor, to spare Akbar's life, but for two years it's been to no avail. Together the two spend time together conspiring different methods of convincing the stubborn doctor the religious merits of forgiveness, and in the process they realize they have more in common than Akbar—they're falling for each other. Mr. Abolqasem's second wife offers a solution: her husband will give clemency if Ala marries her disabled daughter. The choice lies in Ala's hands, but he's not quite sure what to do. Firoozeh removes herself from the decision-making, creating a tension and emotional divide between the two. The film ends ambiguously, as the prison counselor dissuades Mr. Abolqasem from trying to marry off his stepdaughter. Meanwhile, Ala tries to make peace with a reclusive, silent Firoozeh.*

---

The story for *Beautiful City* (*Shah-re Ziba*) began in Farhadi's mind after visiting a courthouse and seeing a bowl moistened with drops of blood, which he later found out was from a recent divorcee who had had trouble removing her wedding ring. As with his other films, Farhadi began with this single, potent image and was compelled to etch in the rest of the story. Using the same metaphor in multiple interviews, he's described the image as "a button for which I needed to buy a suit."[1]

Another inspiration came from Farhadi's daily commute to university in southern Tehran from Isfahan. "I would travel through neighborhoods that had a specific infrastructure and architecture that fit the story that I wanted to tell," he said in an interview after the film's release, noting the heavy presence of metallic structures and steel in the neighborhood (due to nearby railroads). He described these areas of Tehran as "drowning in poverty."[2]

Farhadi originally wrote the screenplay for *Beautiful City* when he was working on a television series, believing the subject of youth penitentiaries would work well with the medium. When TV executives rejected the premise, he shelved the project. Following his first feature, *Dancing in the Dust*, Farhadi returned to make *Beautiful City* into a film. In his own words, Farhadi says he was lucky that his producer, Iraj Taghipour, was willing to produce his second film after *Dancing in the Dust* was financially unsuccessful.

"[Taghipour's] the type of producer who luckily has cultural concerns and not financial ones," Farhadi explained to Iranian press, adding that Taghipour gave the next film his full attention during the production.[3]

*Beautiful City* was Farhadi's first film to play at Tehran's Fajr International Film Festival in February 2004, where it was awarded the Crystal Simorgh for best sound mixing. Outside of the country, his sophomore feature won the Golden Peacock and Special Jury Award (for Faramarz Gharibian's performance) at the International Film Festival of India, as well as the Grand Prix at the Warsaw International Film Festival. The following year, the film also won the FIPRESCI prize at the Split Film Festival.[4]

There were several positive reviews in the West when the film made a short circuit through festivals; it later had a short run at Film Forum in New York City in 2006. Though no one could have guessed it at the time, these critics were essentially announcing the arrival of a fresh new Iranian talent—some also noting the marked difference between Farhadi's style and those of previously revered Iranian auteurs.

Reporting at the Montreal World Film Festival in August 2004, critic Ronnie Scheib explains that the film seemed more accessible to audiences than most "stylistically challenging Farsi fare."[5]

Similarly, *Slant Magazine*'s Ed Gonzalez notes: "Neither unremitting nor detached, [*Beautiful City*] represents something of an anomaly for the Iranian film we're typically used to seeing; its casual manner and openness may or may not win it many fans, but it's this very relaxed vision and delivery that works to legitimize it."[6]

For *The New York Times*, Laura Kern briefly discusses the strength of the performances and script in underscoring the film's resonant themes: "[*Beautiful City*] is neither a prison film . . . nor an inquiry into guilt or innocence. Rather, it's a penetrating exploration of retribution versus forgiveness, blood money, sacrifice and the intricacies of Iran's Islamic judicial system, which places twice as much value on a man's life as on a woman's and permits murderers' death penalties to be lifted only through the request of—and in certain cases, payment from—victims' families."[7]

Though *Beautiful City* tackles serious subject matter, it has several stirring, occasionally mirthful scenes. Its opening is such an example, showcasing the clever and playful pranks adolescents like to play on each other—even if they are at a juvenile delinquent center. A young man named Akbar (Hossein Farzi-Zadeh) is alerted by an inmate that one of their fellow prisoners, Ala (Babak Ansari), has seriously injured himself. Akbar rushes to help and finds Ala lying motionless and unresponsive on his bed. Concerned, Akbar repeatedly calls out his name until the unhurt Ala, calm and collected, turns around with a big smirk on his face. Suddenly boys dash out from all corners of the dormitory and surprise Akbar for his eighteenth birthday. They lift Akbar up and begin to dance and sing. The film's tone collides from fear to defiant jubilation, but not all is well. Though Akbar is delighted to join, he quickly falls out of spiritual sync with the others; soon he is compelled to flee to a washroom in order to privately vent, crying in a bath stall, and when confronted by Ala, Akbar has no words for him—only punches.

Farhadi's narratives typically twist on developments with curious details that leave a trail of questions purposely left unanswered. In *Beautiful City*, the film establishes this elusiveness immediately, and in doing so coaxes the viewer to ask: Why would an eighteen-year-old boy cry during his birthday? Why would he be angry with his friend for organizing a party?

The answer feels like a punch in the gut. A sour-faced Ala asks the equally choleric prison counselor (Farhad Ghaemian) these questions when confronted about the fight. The scolding counselor tells him the obvious truth with deadpan irritation: Now that Akbar is a legal adult he can be executed for his crime. Undoubtedly, the poor boy would not be in the mood to celebrate a marker of life when it is doubly a reminder of his impending death.

Some cultural context is required to understand some of the quick-moving conversations after Ala's reprimand, wherein the boy, the warden, and Ala's counselor talk about "saving" Akbar from corporal punishment. Akbar's execution is a textbook example of *qesas*, a legal concept in Sharia law—practiced in Islamic countries, including Iran—wherein victims' families can choose retribution for a crime against them or a deceased loved one, with the punishment equal to the crime committed (e.g., state execution for a murder offense). Pardoning the criminal and asking for financial restitution (*diyat*) is also an option.[8]

When Ala talks over Akbar's predicament with the warden and counselor, a few things become clear quite quickly: Ala and the counselor do not believe Akbar should die and would like to convince Maliheh's father, Mr. Abolqasem (Faramarz Gharidian), to change his mind, while the mean-spirited warden is less disturbed. He believes in the theory underpinning *qesas*: "Two and two is four. You have to be executed if you kill someone. This is called justice, and the rest is bullshit." He also believes that the father has an immutable stance on the matter—namely, that Akbar should rightly die for killing his daughter.

The viewer only slowly comes to understand the scant details behind the death of the girlfriend Maliheh throughout the film, and as such the film leaves Akbar's crime somewhat ambiguous. The others describe how kind and humane he is, and later the film reveals a few minor details that only make the situation more beguiling: it appears Akbar wanted to kill both himself and Maliheh and she convinced him it only made sense to kill her first. The film does not offer any more information on the circumstances of the murder, suggesting that perhaps Akbar half-botched a suicide pact, or that he was driven to a homicidal and suicidal rage and that in her fear Maliheh consented to be killed. The one thing that does speak to the horror of Akbar's actions is communicated to the viewer by proxy through their respective families' equally impoverished circumstances. Akbar's sister Firoozeh (Taraneh Alidoosti) divorced her drug-abusing husband after she had been driven to prostitute herself in order to support his habit. Maliheh and her father, stepmother, and disabled stepsister are extremely poor in spite of the fact that her father is a doctor. They cannot afford surgery for the stepsister and it is hinted that Mr. Abolqasem had physically abused his own daughter. Because of the slow trickle of this information throughout the film, and because the circumstances of the crime matter less than the aftermath of what happens to Akbar, the film leaves it up the viewer to surmise what may have transpired between Akbar and Maliheh. This is a strategy that Farhadi repeats in later films, most notably in *The Past*, and it forces the viewer, in being unaware of any further details that could clear up Akbar's involvement, to accept the reality that Akbar's punishment more likely than not exceeds his crime (regardless of the viewer's stance on corporal punishment).

Because we come to see Akbar as a caring and considerate prisoner—the counselor compares his long list of good deeds noted by the center to Ala's lack of a similar track record—we accept that the situation involving the murder is undoubtedly more complicated than the film can explain (indeed, it could constitute a whole film by itself) and that Akbar did not kill his girlfriend with any real kind of malice. However, *Beautiful City* prevents us from making any further judgment on the matter. Though the opening scene appears to establish Akbar as the protagonist or at least a main character, the story essentially cuts him out from the rest of the story, even though his impending execution is the catalyst and driving force for all of the developments in the film, as the film's main characters try to save his life.

Akbar's lack of presence once he leaves for the adult penitentiary (which happens within the first five minutes) functionally shapes him into an abstract figure, whose virtue guides and motivates the actions of other characters, particularly Ala, and also Firoozeh, who has been trying to obtain clemency from Mr. Abolqasem since the sentencing. Would it be going too far to describe Akbar as a martyr figure? Perhaps not so strictly in a theological sense, since murder is seen as one of Islam's greatest sins, but Akbar does inspire a moral goodness in people who otherwise have little direction and value in their lives, and his direct absence yet lingering sense of presence—named repeatedly by others in the film—gives him an unmistakable omnipresence, comparable to a religious figure. Akbar is an example of goodness for someone like Ala, imprisoned for thievery.

After sending Akbar to the adult penitentiary, the counselor is determined to once again go ask for clemency from Mr. Abolqasem. But he decides that the fresh-faced and tenacious Ala might have a better chance of dissuading Mr. Abolqasem. Ala, a month away from finishing out his sentence, is given furlough in order to accomplish this difficult task, and the counselor instructs him to obtain the help of Firoozeh.

In introducing the secondary main character, Firoozeh, the film also introduces the sprawling, poverty-stricken parts of town mentioned earlier, which contrast sharply with the strict confines of the juvenile detention center. Space and boundaries increasingly gain meaning throughout the film, as does the manipulative nature of religious rhetoric. This is noticeable in the relationship between the two protagonists and Maliheh's father and stepmother (whom are very religious and poor).

Firoozeh is very assertive in trying to convince the parents to forgive her brother, and in so doing she risks her safety at times, as well as her dignity. The film repeatedly highlights the shame she keeps bringing upon herself. It's noted by Mr. Abolqasem's wife, whose exasperated and apprehensive countenance speaks volumes when Firoozeh shows up at their house for the first time with Akbar: "You're going to be ruded out again. Haven't you taken enough?" But Firoozeh takes it in stride, and here we see a very complicated negotiation taking place between the two women. Firoozeh is stubborn in her attempts, and eventually tires out the wife. Because the woman was only a stepmother figure to Maliheh she is not under the same conviction as her husband, and though she sympathizes to some degree with Firoozeh, she doesn't want to get involved or blamed by Mr. Abolqasem for opening the door to the ever-persistent Firoozeh. The old woman is resigned to the fact that this strange girl will come after her husband and demand clemency up until the minute before Akbar is executed.

It's uncertain if any of the other tactics Firoozeh employs work on the wife, such as when she invokes religious figures. "For the sake of Fatimah Zahra," is one of her first pleading lines to let her into their residence, and it's interesting that in the presence of a woman Firoozeh optimizes her language, employing the name of one of Islam's most respected figures of femininity.[9] And only a few moments later, she repeats herself, this time, "for the sake of the Koran." She also invites Mr. Abolqasem's hatred onto her: "Let him do it, if it makes him feel better." This kind of selflessness cannot be easily dismissed, especially by a religious Iranian woman who feels the pressure of Iranian etiquette (*taarof*) to be gracious, even to strangers.

Firoozeh repeats this strategy once seated inside with the seemingly reproachful but silent Mr. Abolqasem, and when she unveils her latest present for his family (some kind of ceramic decoration) he threatens her immediately to take it away—even after she explains that there is a Koran on top of it. Unlike his wife, Mr. Abolqasem is resistant to her reasoning. When she tries to explain that Akbar has just turned eighteen and has "suffered the equivalent of ten executions in the past two years," he begins to lose his temper, finally erupting when Firoozeh claims that Maliheh wouldn't want Akbar's death. He kicks her out—literally—and thus angers a bewildered Ala.

Though she's hurt, Firoozeh refuses to lose her calm and is barely troubled by the failure of their attempt—as if she's suffered the same abuse countless times before (indeed, earlier in the film she mentions a month-long headache after her last encounter with Mr. Abolqasem). There is a considerable degree of tension between Firoozeh and Ala after this encounter. Later, on the bus ride home, she confides to him, "I'm willing to do anything for Akbar: to belittle myself, to be cursed, to beg, and to lie. But I don't want anyone to see me that way."

The film has this wonderful, subversive outlook on Firoozeh's strong-willed actions, demanding a feminist reading. No matter how many times she goes after the parents for clemency, no matter how many times she's rebuffed and hurt by the old couple, she comes off as simultaneously assertive and altruistic, never shameful. In so doing, her actions reveal the injustice to which women are regarded in Iranian society and the way in which we view them as precious, delicate beings that ought to be protected from disgrace, instead of individuals with their own agency. When Firoozeh becomes active and tenacious, she sacrifices her own credibility for the love of her brother and his life. It's this act of altruism that truly undermines the social stigma she's supposed to feel.

Ala is the next one to act—and he decides to do it alone. He writes a letter to Mr. Abolqasem pretending to be Akbar requesting redemption, and then gives it to the doctor, acting as if the mail had to be delivered personally. Mr. Abolqasem first thinks he's a patient, but when the boy begins to read the letter aloud, Mr. Abolqasem's demeanor quickly changes from one of gracious host to quiet indignation. He leaves while Ala is still reading.

Yet Ala is not done with him, and in one of the film's few moments of hilarity, Mr. Abolqasem finds himself being stalked by Ala. While shaking hands with fellow prayers at a mosque, the camera follows his eyes as he connects his hands with another man. A medium shot reveals the stranger to be none other than the relentless Ala, whose presence nonplusses the previously serene Mr. Abolqasem. Ala is clearly only there to demonstrate his own seriousness about religion, and like Firoozeh, Ala wants to appeal to Mr. Abolqasem on the same page. And though the film never seems to spell out how devout Ala or Firoozeh are—their lower class would predict that they would be, but that's only a generalization—it's clear that religion does not dictate their lives on the same level as Mr. Abolqasem or his wife. Outside of their conversations with the older couple, the two protagonists do not speak religiously. This makes it a lot more likely that they are using the logic of Islam's dogma as a means of persuasion.

Several scenes later, the film exposes the extent to which the incentive for clemency is institutionalized. Sharia law claims that the life of a woman is deemed to be worth half of a man's. Mr. Abolqasem must produce blood money to Akbar's kin to make up this difference in order for Akbar to be executed in a prompt fashion. But Mr. Abolqasem, despite being a doctor, is extremely poor, and is thus unable to pay this money, leaving Akbar in an imprisoned existential limbo.

Mr. Abolqasem questions the imposed limitations in front of a judge and imam. "He killed my daughter. . . . But I have to pay in order for him to be executed?" he asks the cleric incredulously. To Mr. Abolqasem, the notion that his daughter's life is worth so little is inane, and he expresses his argument sharply: "My girl's life is worth half of that bastard's life?"

In having an extremely pious character doubt the so-deemed logic of the religious law, the film reveals the chasms in Sharia law and the disadvantages of being poor and Muslim. Despite the correlation between religiosity and poverty—which is true in Iran insofar as many lower-class citizens tend to fall more on the fundamentalist side—*Beautiful City* posits that religion doesn't always serve its most loyal demographic all too kindly. Mr. Abolqasem truly believes in his right to seek vengeance for his daughter's death and the law permits him to do so, but at a great cost that seems out of sync with his own values.

"The same religion you believe in is hasty when it comes to someone being killed by another. So it puts barriers in your way so you will forgive instead," explains the imam. Though forgiveness is encouraged by God, Mr. Abolqasem remains unconvinced that his every action should surmount to charity when it's linked so closely to his socio-economic status. "One thing us poor people have a lot of in this world is doing good deeds, sir," he tells the imam.

For Muslims, the concept of doubt (*shak*) is an important factor in making difficult decisions, and the Koran has lengthy explanations on what kind of decisions one is able to make with or without the presence of doubt. Mr. Abolqasem encounters this challenge when the imam explains the virtues of forgiveness. He becomes conflicted over his certainty. Yet the religious weight of his decision becomes undone when money enters the picture.

Mr. Abolqasem's wife comes up with a solution for Ala and Firoozeh, which she claims she can get Mr. Abolqasem to buy if their imam helps them. Her disabled daughter (Mr. Abolqasem's stepdaughter) is in need of surgery, and if the two can come up with the blood money, she'll convince her husband to take it.

Naturally, Firoozeh cannot make pay the money upfront, and the plan falls apart. The wife's second solution, however, causes an emotional quagmire between the two protagonists. She proposes that Ala marry off her daughter, thereby ensuring her future (the disabled daughter is treated as some kind of property that can be pawned off, even for something as serious as religious clemency). The casualness with which the characters discuss this solution normalizes its inherent ridiculousness, but what's more bewildering for Ala and Firoozeh is how it will affect them—now that they've both slyly hinted that they like each other.

The film slowly trickles this narrative information throughout the film by way of a few small moments that range from simple (like Firoozeh putting more attention into her appearance before seeing Ala) to symbolic (like the scene mentioned earlier in which Firoozeh tries to remove her stubbornly wedged wedding ring). These gestures all follow a long, leisurely restaurant conversation between the two young adults in which their undeniable chemistry seeps through the typical parameters of Iranian artistic censorship. The only sliver of tension arises when Ala denies Firoozeh a cigarette. "I don't like women who smoke."

Should Firoozeh let Ala marry another woman, or let her brother die just so she can be with him? The implications of her decision are too overwhelming, and she decides that she must remove herself from the situation. Ala is more straightforward about his response—naturally, he doesn't want to accept the proposition because he likes Firoozeh, but he also doesn't want his best friend to die. When he tries to confirm that the two have feelings for each other, Firoozeh closes up like a clam, further conflicting Ala.

This development forces a narrative impasse, and the film closes on a beguiling ambiguity. Like with so many other Farhadian characters, Ala and Firoozeh are forced to choose between their desires and immutable reality. Sitting in her apartment, ignoring Ala's knocks at her door, Firoozeh quietly puffs on a cigarette—the same habit he had reprimanded her for earlier in the film, when things were more simple. Will she answer the door? Maybe.

## Fireworks Wednesday

*The Day I Became A Woman*

> It would be nice to be able to take a motorbike ride in the mountains feeling so close to the person sitting next to you, yet neither the traditionalist past nor the modern future leave much room for remaining sincere and genuine in relationships even with those within arm's reach. So, the journey must continue. – Anton Oleinik[1]

*A recently engaged lower-class woman, Rouhi (Taraneh Alidoosti), receives a cleaning assignment at an upper-middle-class residence from her employment agency on Fireworks Wednesday, one of the most festive and busiest holidays in Iran. Upon arrival, she realizes that the chaotic mess in the apartment matches the dynamic of the family; the constantly rowing couple, Morteza (Hamid Farokhnezhad) and Mojdeh (Hediyeh Tehrani), can't even agree on whether or not Rouhi should be cleaning the apartment. Mojdeh suspects her husband is cheating on her with their next-door neighbor Simine (Pantea Bahram), and asks Rouhi to act as her spy to gain information, an operation the young, innocent servant botches more than once. When Mojdeh finally takes matters into her own hands and steals Rouhi's chador to sneak out and spy on her husband, he attacks her and is disgraced in front of his coworkers. For most of the narrative the implication is that Mojdeh is acting overly paranoid, though near the end the film confesses to Morteza and Simine's illicit affair, when the two meet clandestinely in a car. When Rouhi brings Morteza's child back from the celebrations, she smells Simine's perfume in the car, deducing that Morteza is, indeed, committing adultery. She attempts to communicate the information to Mojdeh, but only gets so far as raising the wife's suspicions once again. The film concludes with Rouhi being reunited with her fiancé before they drive home together. After her tumultuous day, Rouhi is now a changed woman, understanding exactly what her marriage may hold in store.*

---

Beginning with his third film, Asghar Farhadi focused his stories increasingly on the experience of middle-class Iranians—a move that, in retrospect, was smartly planned and fortuitous given the director's later successes.

"With *Fireworks Wednesday*, I started becoming increasingly influenced by what actually went on in my own life," he clarified in an interview. "Another reason when I thought about the shift later . . . is that in the modern world the destiny of a society is determined by its middle class. I wanted to discuss this tier of the society more. The great thing about middle-class stories is that you can at once discuss other rungs of the society."[2]

Indeed, Farhadi's later films feature at least one poor character who marks the contrast between the different classes. Within Farhadi's oeuvre, *Fireworks Wednesday* is the work that most equally balances its concerns between the upper and lower classes. The protagonist, Rouhi, is a young servant-for-hire, and the story is mostly based around her point-of-view as a fresh-faced neophyte in the world of marriage and adulthood. But what she gains in perspective throughout the film is not quite a glimpse into the allegedly more sophisticated upper-class existence, but a reality that is disappointingly based on duplicity, operating with a moral relativism she cannot fully navigate within the systems of knowledge provided to her through school and religion.

*Fireworks Wednesday* also features a second writing credit: Mani Haghighi, an Iranian actor/director who performed in Farhadi's *About Elly*. The two developed the story together in a rather idiosyncratic manner. In fact, it was strange that Farhadi collaborated on a writing project at all after his experience making *Dancing in the Dust* (for which he co-wrote the screenplay). Because he'd felt that the story for *Dancing in the Dust* had not come directly from within him, at that point in time Farhadi had decided to work individually on his own ideas.

Everything changed when, one night while spending time with Haghighi, their conversation gravitated towards Farhadi's latest script, a work-in-progress. "The next morning when we woke up, we called each other and started talking again and after a few months, it automatically felt like we were working together," he explained.

This collaboration was purely incidental but ultimately fruitful—not in spite of, but *due to* their constant arguments. "We rarely agreed on anything. If I had an idea, I had to reason with him and convince him why it was good and vice versa. We were continuously arguing with each other and fighting. It was a constructive experience."[3]

This would not be the last time the two worked together. Farhadi co-wrote Haghighi's *Canaan* in 2008. The film is about a woman about to divorce her husband and leave the country, but who is moored in doubt about her latter decision when other family issues arise. In some ways, *Canaan*'s premise anticipates *A Separation* by a few years.

The family melodrama of *Fireworks Wednesday* allowed the filmmaker to make several comments on the state of marriage in Iranian society and its impact on women, whether they were married, soon-to-be-wed, or divorced. The film is particularly realistic in the way in which it portrays the role of deception in relationships, and how lying becomes normalized between partners, frequently resulting in a complete breakdown in communication. The reason why Morteza and Mojdeh cannot settle their problems is a complete lack of trust in one another, resulting in desperate measures taken to spy on, abuse and shame each other.

Though the relationship is toxic—which is unsurprisingly wreaking havoc on their son's well-being—it's also an extreme example that is purposely set as a contrast to the new relationship between servant-for-hire Rouhi and her fiancé. Rouhi couldn't be more excited about her imminent nuptials, and her dynamic with her fiancé is loving and blissful. Indeed, the couple are still in the honeymoon phase of their period. But Rouhi changes, ever so slightly, after being assigned to clean Morteza and Mojdeh's house and becoming complicit in their marital equivalent of a cold war. The film never emphasizes her epiphany about marriage. As one of many subtle touches in the film, it appears as a slight glimmer in her eyes when she reunites with her fiancé. The story instead devotes most of its running time to a detailed account of her tumultuous, never-ending day.

The film takes place on Fireworks Wednesday (*Chaharshanbe Souri*), one of the most celebratory days of the year, which prepares people for the Persian New Year (*Nowruz*). Taking place on the eve of the last Wednesday of the year, Iranians jump over bonfires, throw huge street parties, and set off firecrackers. They divine their fortune from overheard conversations. While the origins of the celebration are Zoroastrian, its importance as a purification ritual (which symbolizes the cleansing power of fire, preparing participants for the new year) is viewed less religiously—people of all faiths celebrate Fireworks Wednesday.[4]

As if to demonstrate the degree to which the young couple's relationship is free of trouble, the film establishes early on how tensions are easily mitigated. The excessive fabric from Rouhi's chador becomes entangled in the motorbike, forcing them to make a quick emergency stop. But it doesn't take long before the couple regains their good spirits. "I told you to be careful with your chador," he initially reprimands her, but we never know if it's because Rouhi is being careless or if the exorbitant length of the chador is simply not designed for motorcycle wear. "I don't understand why you even need to wear it out here. Who's going to see you?"

This line, though offhanded, may seem like an obvious bit of social critique (and only a minute into the film!), but the screenplay quickly moves on, as if the comment were completely innocuous and casual. Indeed, the script downplays the significance through humor: Rouhi peskily replies, "You!" at the exact moment the fiancé is comically thrown back onto the ground as he successfully untangles the chador. The two delve into laughter and a snowball fight, and order is restored.

Because this scene is so strikingly similar to an opening vignette in Farhadi's first film, *Dancing in the Dust*, it demonstrates the filmmaker's growth as a storyteller. *Dancing in the Dust* begins with a series of quick scenes about the blossoming love between a young couple, but it uses a fair bit of pronounced foreshadowing to spell out their impending trouble, including a tarot reading and the male protagonist asking his wife the extremes to which she would go to prove his love to him.

Like both *Dancing in the Dust* and Farhadi's second film, *Beautiful City*, *Fireworks Wednesday* garnered several awards in its run on the festival circuit in 2006. Notably, at Fajr, the film won three Crystal Simorghs: Farhadi for best director, Hediyeh Tehrani for best actress, and Hayedeh Safiyari for best editing. At Kerala International Film Festival, Farhadi won the Silver Crow Pheasant for best director; at the Chicago International Film Festival, the film won the Gold Hugo for best feature; and at Locarno, it won second place for the Youth Jury Award, and Farhadi was nominated for the Golden Leopard. In 2007, *Fireworks Wednesday* won the Golden Lady Harimaguada at the Las Palmas Film Festival.[5]

Reception was generally positive. With *Fireworks Wednesday*, an increasing number of critics began to point out Farhadi's capabilities in crafting an enticing middle-class melodrama—a genre that Deborah Young noted was missing from most Iranian films (more accurately for those films distributed internationally). "Few Iranian films have tried to realistically depict both the urban middle and lower classes, and fewer still with the complexity of story telling and depth of characterization in Asghar Farhadi's impressive third feature," she wrote in her *Variety* review.[6]

More recognition came in years to come, when the film was re-released on DVD in Europe following the international successes of *A Separation* and *The Past*. Cinephiles curious about Farhadi's earlier output were given the opportunity to discover it anew.

"As with his other films, Farhadi shows an icily cool control in his camerawork, comparable to a Haneke, especially in the gripping street-brawl scene, blankly filmed from an ascending lift," concludes Peter Bradshaw in his DVD review for *The Guardian*.[7]

Farhadi's vastly improved visual language in *Fireworks Wednesday* also helps to shape his nearly invisible cultural critique. Though his two first films were more remarkable than most reviews let on, the works did consist mostly of safe, predictable compositions and camera angles, sometimes swaying towards too-conspicuous symbolism. However, this is not to suggest that with *Fireworks Wednesday* (and onward) Farhadi abandoned his previous style and opted for something more flamboyant. What develops with his third film is a natural refinement of style.

One fascinating exception that does fall on the side of flamboyance is the scene mentioned by Bradshaw. More than halfway through the film, Mojdeh fibs to Rouhi that she plans to nap and asks her to pick up her son Amir-Ali from school. When Rouhi goes to leave she finds her chador missing, and then when trying to locate Mojdeh in the apartment realizes the woman has left.

Mojdeh has stolen the chador in order to spy on her husband and see if Morteza has actually gone to work like he'd said. However, he's tipped off when the school calls him and asks if it's okay for Rouhi to take his son home. He immediately suspects his wife has come to check up on him and spies from his office window. Upon spotting her, he takes the elevator down to accost her, and ends up hitting her in public.

This violent confrontation is framed through the glass elevator's window, which shows the exterior of the building. We are with Morteza as he gets on, but the camera remains static after he gets off, and as the elevator ascends we are given a glimpse of their encounter. The window is slightly smeared and cracked at the bottom of the elevator, so our view is not perfectly visible, but we see enough to witness the aftermath of Morteza's anger and the necessity for bystanders to get involved to protect Mojdeh.[8] All the while, the elevator music—almost saccharine-sweet in its pleasantness—both tempers the ugliness of the violent outburst and suggests something more symbolic and accusatory of Iranian society.[9] By denying the viewer a clear view of the couple's row, the film suggests the hidden side of domestic abuse in the country. Despite its prevalence, domestic abuse is regularly hidden. In Iran, violence against women and children is a systemic phenomenon fuelled by tradition and religion, and supported by an authoritarian state that denies women the same rights as men.[10]

This is a feminist interpretation—not one that Farhadi necessarily planned—but even if he did, an Iranian filmmaker can only make such an argument with certain caveats—namely, ensuring that the unlucky perpetrators in this film lack religious devotion, all thanks to their selfish, secular, upper-class existence (there are numerous other instances of the film pointing out their solipsism, like the irritated school principal who doesn't buy Rouhi's excuse that Mojdeh was busy). Not only does the film balance its societal critique, it conveys the notion that not only poor women are affected by violence (a reminder is also present in *About Elly*, when Amir abuses Sepideh). Equally shocking is the cavalier attitudes of men in the aftermath. Though Morteza's actions are deemed shameful by everyone around him—in his subsequent conversation with his shocked boss he apologizes for his behavior and claims it's the first time—these characters, as well as the cab driver who takes a crying Mojdeh home, implicitly justify Morteza's actions and suggest the couple "solve" their problems at home.

In *Fireworks Wednesday*, it's quite apparent that Farhadi has begun to understand the importance of physical space in creating his highly charged visuals. The elevator keeps us deliberately removed from the action. Elsewhere, physical occlusions serve other purposes, like in an early scene where Rouhi tries on her wedding dress (on loan from a coworker who also offers alterations). She can only catch a glimpse of her figure in the dress from a tiny little compact mirror, and when the coworker checks up on her in the bathroom the door is cracked halfway open, as if no one can be allowed a full view of the wife-to-be. This might suggest the purity of unmarried women but it might also suggest that Rouhi has not yet transformed into the fully self-realized adult she will become upon entering marriage.

The wedding dress visuals show up elsewhere, when Rouhi is taking care of the apartment's white and lacy curtains. She closes the drapes, opens others, takes some of them down; in her hands she looks like she's holding a wedding dress. These actions signal her own maturation as a young woman who remains in a liminal state in which she's confused about how to live her life. Complementing this visual motif are two other reminders of marriage. First is the beautiful glassware on the dining room table where she frequently moves around—likely a wedding gift from Morteza and Mojdeh's youth. The way the glasses adorn the table are also reminiscent of the traditional wedding spread in Persian weddings (*sofreh-yeh Agh'd*). The second visual reminder are the virginal-white blankets veiling the furniture for Mojdeh's planned painting job.

The apartment is the film's most important physical space, and it's clear that many of the innovative visuals seen in *A Separation* began with Farhadi's experimentation in this film. The family's place is a mess, an obvious metaphor for the state of the couple's relationship, but it's amazing how compelling this setting works to establish the moods of the characters. There is one notable long take of the apartment wherein a calm Morteza is seen in the distance puffing on a cigarette and looking out the window, the smoke travelling around the domestic chaos. Similarly, another silent shot finds an immobile Mojdeh sitting at the table. Her back is to the camera (like Morteza's in the other shot), and one can only imagine she is contemplative of the mess around her—in both its physical and psychological manifestations.

The film also features another typical Farhadian touch: a cinematic and memorable shot serving the opening credits. In her coverage for Tribeca, Sheila O'Malley listed *Fireworks Wednesday* as her favorite film of the festival, describing the significance of this sequence:

> "... [T]he charm of *Fireworks Wednesday* is not in an innovative story. It is in scenes like the one where Roohi sits on a bus, going to her temp agency to get an assignment, and puts her hand out the window. The music is in a melancholy minor key, a direct contrast to the giggly light-hearted mood of the pre-credits sequence on the motorcycle. We can see her billowing black sleeve and a pale hand swimming its way through the air. There is love here, and expectation, and a sense of looking-forward-to-things, but deep crevasses also exist, there is always an undercurrent of potential loss."[11]

O'Malley points out two remarkable elements in *Fireworks Wednesday*. Firstly, the film's textured storytelling, aided by subtle foreshadowing. The film progresses in meticulously laid-out layers to make its thesis about the complexity of marriage, and its opening scenes are paramount to achieving this effect. But while the film builds in layers and complexity, it also underscores its conspicuously marked storyline—one that is structured deliberately as a full-circle loop. The film begins with Rouhi being dropped off by her fiancé before she encounters an incredibly overwhelming and tumultuous day that will forever change her expectations about married life. The film ends with the couple being reunited so he can drive her home. The film begins with Rouhi's innocence and ends with her maturation. She may not be married yet, but after witnessing and becoming involved in the intricate dynamics between Mojdeh and Morteza, Rouhi becomes a changed woman. She *is* now a woman. All the little touches in these opening scenes spell her bright and happy future, but they are tinged with some deeper sentiment—a kind of futilistic, cynical outlook on the fate that awaits not only Rouhi, but anyone who will experience marriage.

Regarding those opening credits, it's important to establish how seemingly innocuous Rouhi's hand and wisp of scarf flowing out the wind seem in relation to their temporal position in the film. The fact that this image coincides with the credits undermine the significance of the imagery, but one thing that does tip off the viewer of its thematic import is the boldness of the camera movements that leads up to the hand coming out the window; they seem downright grandiose for Farhadi's style. Positioned inside a bus by the doors, the camera remains static as the roaming bus reveals patches of a street as if in fast-forward. One of the pedestrians that runs by is Rouhi, then a jump cut shows the bus slowed down at a stop where a crowd of travellers await for the doors open. Faces and figures move close to the camera as the passengers step up past the camera, with Rouhi the last to get on. The beautiful, bleak score begins, and the next shot reveals the bus window from the outside. The sunlight reflected on the glass darkens everything inside, revealing instead fleeting glimpses of the street's architecture. The window is slightly open, allowing Rouhi's hand to escape alongside a bunch of her chador fabric, which flows in tandem with her hand, sufficiently relaxed so as to wave and flutter to the force and whim of the wind. The credits begin and are elegantly poised to the right of this composition.

*Fireworks Wednesday* thus signals Farhadi's transition from heavy-handed symbolism into something more subtle. Everyday objects like windows, doorframes, chadors, and family photo albums are shown occasionally, but never obtrusively in the viewer's eye, and sometimes these shots are held for such a long period of time the viewer feels compelled to think more deeply about what they are seeing. The small fragment of chador flowing freely out the window is one such example; on the one hand, there is almost nothing extraordinary about the fact that Rouhi would put her hand out the window to feel the touch of the wind. Yet focusing on this small moment for such a long period of time during the credits sequence—especially after the chador has already made itself into something like a secondary character after the motorbike incident—compels the viewer to think of its presence in the lives of Iranian women, and by proxy, their male partners.

Repetition is useful for this approach. The chador shows up again and again in the film, serving more than one narrative purpose. It goes without saying that part of the reason this symbolism is so effective in its near-invisibility is due to censorship. Though the fiancé's comment in the first scene seems like an exemplary line that would have and should have been scratched out by the more religious censors working on this script, the line also carries a sense of innocuous irreproachability. The fiancé doesn't seem to be blaming religion for forcing Rouhi to wear a chador everywhere. He just questions the practicality of it when there is no one around to see his wife. It's not intended to be a larger statement about the restrictive livelihood of women in Iran, because it comes off like a common expression and complaint (to those living outside of Iran, the statement may seem more meaningful when in actuality, given the context, it's not).

The treatment of the chador as a necessary garb is also presented in the film elsewhere, thus balancing and neutralizing these kinds of comments. An example is a scene halfway through the film, when a chador-less Rouhi calls her fiancé from the family's balcony in order to let him know she'll be late (she leaves a message with his colleague, which is ultimately never delivered). A neighboring teenage boy spies on her from his window and openly flirts with Rouhi, as if the missing chador were an invitation. This embarrasses poor Rouhi but also calls into question the value and importance of the chador in Iranian society. Given its prohibitive nature on women, the chador has conditioned Iranian men to treat women differently—without it, women are deemed less pure and thus subjugated to all kinds of sexual harassment. With or without the chador, Iranian women are moored to unrealistic expectations of how they should exist in public domains, which is all the more oppressive than simply being forced to wear one. That's a much more complicated and nuanced feminist argument than simply challenging the forced existence of the chador, and one of the main reasons why Farhadi's film works so well.

The hegemonic power of the chador cannot be escaped even by Rouhi, who feels unsafe without one. After leaving the family's apartment, she is nearly run over by an ungainly skateboarder who was clearly getting close to her on purpose. Under her breath she calls him a jerk before seeing Morteza arrive home. "I left my chador at your place," she explains to him. "I feel too embarrassed to go upstairs again. Can you please get it for me?"

Given the events that transpired earlier—namely, Mojdeh's spying—the narrative charges the chador with a kind of cosmic irony. It is a symbol of oppression and a necessity for women's safety, certainly; but alternately, the privacy it gives women can be used by them for purposes of surveillance. In a film that speaks so eloquently about duplicity in marriage, the chador registers as a kind of secret weapon, though this is neither tinged as positive or negative. In *Fireworks Wednesday*, the chador simply *exists*; it's an instrument enforced for religious purposes that can gain new social uses and implementations that reflect the society at large. Some women have turned hijab-wear into fashion statements in the absence of showing off their beauty, while others, like Mojdeh, have reconstructed their chadors to perpetuate paranoia.

This latter repurposing also correlates with other social circumstances specific to Iran—for example, the extreme punishment given to adulterers. Morteza, despite the fact that he is indeed cheating on his wife and desires to leave her for Simine, would not be able to bring himself to confess to his crime or divorce Mojdeh. Even middle-class Iranians look down on divorce, and the consequences that it has on familial dynamics is seen as tragic and destructive. The film acknowledges this reality with its melancholic ending, which includes long takes of individual characters who are not celebrating Fireworks Wednesday together in a family unit. They are separate, quiet, and unhappy. Morteza has a run-in with Simine's ex-husband, who has dropped off their daughter at her mother's house for a visit. When Morteza returns home and finds the ex napping in his car while awaiting his daughter's return, he is compelled to invite the man inside to his own apartment. One can sense that Morteza feels this hospitality is a karmic gesture of sorts, as if he can provide the man a chance to celebrate Fireworks Wednesday with a surrogate family, which thereby forces Morteza's own family to pretend they are normal and happy in the stranger's presence—but the man resists. When Morteza returns to his home, he finds Mojdeh asleep with Amir Ali in his child-sized bed and is unable to wake her. So he lies alone in a bed that seems too large, visibly empty without his wife. Then we see Mojdeh's eyes open briefly—she was pretending to be asleep so that she wouldn't have to put up with her husband, and we know this marriage will not last. Will they go on their vacation tomorrow? Possibly—possibly not—but it shall inspire yet another round of arguments. The vicious cycle goes on.

## About Elly

*Secrets and Lies*

*A group of friends take a trip to the north of Iran for a three-day vacation at a beach house. Three couples and their children are reunited with their longtime friend Ahmad, recently divorced and returned from Germany. One of the women, unofficial ringleader Sepideh, also invites along Elly, her daughter's schoolteacher. Sepideh has coaxed the reticent Elly into coming in order to meet Ahmad in a persistent effort to play matchmaker (she even lies to the housekeeper in order to obtain a villa, explaining that Ahmad and Elly are newlyweds). The friends have all known each other since law school, whereas Elly is an outsider, understandably feeling out of place with the crew's inside jokes and raillery. It doesn't help that the others subconsciously treat her as an inferior, and she is quick to exercise deferential politeness and obliged to play the part of servant. Though their humor is all in good fun, Elly is increasingly embarrassed the more she overhears their jokes about Ahmad. She insists she must leave after one night to take care of her ailing mother. Undeterred, the stubborn Sepideh hides Elly's bag to stop her. Nearly half the film is devoted to establishing the dynamics between the friends and witnessing their games and casual conversations—it's the calm before*

the storm. While the men play volleyball and the women are out on errands, Elly babysits the three children. Suddenly two of the kids alert their parents that the third, Arash, is drowning in the water, and the men and lifeguards frantically dive into the water and save the boy. But Elly is also missing, and unlike Arash, she cannot be found. The friends do everything in their power to save her, admonishing the authorities for not searching the water thoroughly, and stress over how to confront Elly's family, suddenly realizing no one—even Sepideh—knows her last name. They are besought by unanswerable questions, even suspecting that Elly may not have drowned—perhaps their ridicule forced her to leave. Upon tracking down a man who claims to be her brother, Sepideh is forced to come clean about one crucial bit of information: Elly, a single child, was trying to break things off with her fiancé Alireza (he pretended to be her brother in order to reach her). Suddenly, the crew's leisurely tomfoolery—taking Elly on vacation with strange men, and treating Ahmad and Elly as newlyweds—takes on a degree of devastating gravitas as they try to manage Alireza's understanding and handling of what transpired. Having lied numerous times throughout the film, Sepideh wants to be upfront with Alireza and explain that she was the only one who knew Elly was engaged—but everyone refuses, arguing that Alireza won't believe her and find them all culpable. Eventually, Sepideh conforms, telling the shaken Alireza that Elly never mentioned him. The film ends with the devastated Alireza identifying Elly's body at the morgue.

---

*About Elly* (*Darbareye Elly*), one of Farhadi's true masterpieces, was lauded at the time of its release in 2009 and re-appraised further in 2011 and 2012 following the success of *A Separation*. And rightly so: the film, about a group of young, upper-middle-class Tehranis vacationing in the north, is a tightly structured screenplay subtly critical of that tier in society, operating within a Hitchcockian narrative logic, framed and shot with rarefied vision, and following a taut, kinetic rhythm.

Like *A Separation*, *About Elly* reveals a society built on deception and suspicion, but it never lays blame on any particular individual. Of all of Farhadi's films, however, *About Elly* is perhaps the closest work that comes to being outright in its criticisms of Iran's secular middle-class. But because this is a Farhadi film, nothing is ever spelled out.

"It's a shame that it's taken such a monumental accolade for Farhadi's fourth feature to see the light of day," observed Patrick Gamble for *CineVue* in 2012,[1] after the film made its official theatrical release in the UK. Gamble wasn't the only one to notice.[2] Indeed, the comment echoed one made by Jens Hinrichsen the year prior, who noted in *Film-Dienst* that the film's 2011 release in Germany came two years after Farhadi had won the Silver Bear for Best Director at Berlinale.[3]

*About Elly*'s initial release in 2009 had also faced delays when it became mired in some controversy with the Iranian government. There were reports that the authorities wanted to censor the film in Iran due to the presence of its star, Golshifteh Farahani, who had been banned from returning home after acting in Ridley Scott's *Body of Lies*. Farhadi and Farahani denied the rumors, and the film's screenings went as planned in early 2009, when it played at Fajr and Berlinale.[4]

At Fajr, the film won the Audience Award for best film, Farhadi picked up a Crystal Simorgh for best director, and Hassan Zahedi was awarded a Crystal Simorgh for best sound. At Tribeca, *About Elly* won best narrative feature; at Viennale, it received the Standard Readers' Jury Award. The film also picked up awards at the Asia Pacific Screen Awards, Asia-Pacific Film Festival, Brisbane International Film Festival, and Kerala International Film Festival. The film garnered eight award nominations at other festivals.[5]

The light attention it did receive upon its debut at festivals was mixed. For *Variety*, Alissa Simon flagged *About Elly*'s first act as more cloying than entertaining. "To many, the film's first half may seem mannered, even boring, with the old pals, particularly the men, indulging in obnoxious, condescending behavior. But after an alarming incident at the 45-minute mark, Farhadi ratchets up the tension, and the pic becomes a mystery thriller of sorts that epitomizes the Sir Walter Scott quote, 'Oh what a tangled web we weave, when first we practice to deceive.' "[6]

Part of the appeal of the film, however, lay in its representation of the Iranian middle-class in an internationally released film. Parviz Jahed noted this focus in Farhadi's work: "The young, educated and middle-class travellers in the film are somewhat of an unknown demographic to a western audience."[7]

The adverse reaction of a few critics to the characters' tomfoolery may be bound in a cultural barrier, but there's also a possibility that the banality of the characters' fun is purposeful, underscoring the lack of discreet charms of the Iranian bourgeoisie.

Some reviews compared the film to those by European masters.[8] Its regularly cited similarity to Michelango Antonioni's *L'Avventura*—the films share a similar premise, about the aftermath of a woman who goes mysteriously missing at a secluded beachside—was too easy to ignore, but it's a superficial connection at best. Though the two share this distinct narrative, Farhadi's intentions and style could not be further removed from Antonioni's. One is interested in the complexity of interpersonal dynamics and their breakdown with a fast rhythm and expansive script to match; the other finds those threads less interesting than the insular alienation of its characters, reveling instead in cold lugubriousness.

Despite *About Elly*'s theatrical delay throughout most of the world—it is available on DVD, at any rate—the reviews picked up steam after the release of its successor, *A Separation*.

In *Sight & Sound*, Philip Kemp noted the visual symmetry between action, its accompanying tensions and their representation onscreen: "Farhadi's camerawork mirrors this intricate complex of deceit, often roaming around the villa in long unbroken takes, picking out expressions of resentment or mistrust, flitting from one character to another as if weaving the skein of untruths that binds them unhappily together as the mood darkens towards final desolation."[9]

Parviz Jahed compared this camerawork to that of John Cassavetes: "[T]he camera almost never closes in on their faces, picturing them often in long or medium shot. Even Elly, the main character of the film, is rarely the point of focus of the camera's attention and is often seen in a crowd or in the margins of the frame."[10]

This visually alienating effect correlates with the film's deeper cultural subtext about communal deception. When lies are slowly revealed one by one by different characters, we come to realize the pervasive need to lie for these characters, who, for 45 minutes, have demonstrated an ostensibly close-knit alliance.

"It's easy to see *About Elly* as a film criticising the culture of deception in Iranian society, but Farhadi keeps such political commentary as subtext," argued Phil Concannon, for *Little White Lies*. "First and foremost, his film is a gripping human drama, one that poses serious moral questions while challenging our preconceptions at every turn."[11]

The film's thriller/mystery genre elements work to both involve the viewer and elide its lambast of the middle class. The degree to which Farhadi slyly sneaks in this social subtext is apparent even with the film's opening image—the near-black interior of a charity box—but it's so fleeting it's easily missable (or forgettable). Light streams in through the box slit, illuminating the passage of some bills into the abyss. The imagery is perplexing, given that it's disconnected from everything else to follow. The thin rectangle of light then transforms from a box slit into the light visible at end of a car tunnel, and the darkness begins to wash away as the camera gets closer and closer to the sunlight, revealing cars full of exuberant young people yelling and screaming with joy. Their shrieks are defiant and raucous, as though they've really earned their vacation, but within the tunnel the screams become ghoulish, taking on a terrifying tinge. Like with *Fireworks Wednesday*, the tiniest narrative details foreshadow what's to come in such a gradual and textured manner that it's easy to ignore or forget about them during a first-time viewing.

*About Elly*'s first act operates like a casual travelogue, as if promoting the idyll of Shomal. A passenger-side view from the car shows one public park after another dotted with colorful tents as the crew gets closer and closer to its destination.

It becomes apparent very quickly that Sepideh, the group leader, has a penchant for lying, and though she's aware of it she remains oblivious to the harm her deceit can cause. She is the reason why they're denied a villa upon their arrival near the Caspian Sea. The house-sitter had explained that they were fully booked when she spoke to Sepideh on the phone, but the young wife decided to try her luck anyway, dragging along the whole crew without telling them they might be out of luck.

Though a few express irritation—particularly Sepideh's husband, Amir—a solution does present itself: an abandoned and dirty house is available right by the beachside. They leisurely stroll in and start planning how to use the space. The kids find their place immediately, beginning to run around the beach and play in the water. Elly is inclined to offer her services—cleaning, taking care of the kids—and though this is part etiquette, being busy also gives her a chance to disappear into another room when the friends become overly jovial. When the men start goofing off and dancing, for example, she's clearly uncomfortable in their presence. It's also important to underline the Islamic element for her shyness—as an unmarried woman, she technically shouldn't be watching men perform like that, especially without a male companion and especially in front of strangers (though most secular Iranian women wouldn't care).

The group's swift conversational rhythm reveals Sepideh's last-minute scheming. Ahmad has recently returned from Germany after divorcing his wife. Sepideh invited Elly along to introduce the two and see how they fare together—a fact the rest of the group already knows or quickly discovers. Ahmad becomes an easy target for his jokes, but because it begins to involve Elly the humor, though good-hearted, starts to gently rouse Elly's nerves. We barely see this taking place other than her occasional forced, polite smile (that more accurately resembles a grimace) or when she stalls in the kitchen after offering to retrieve salt for their meal.

She informs Sepideh that she must leave after the first night to take care of her mother (who recently suffered a heart attack), but Sepideh demurs and brushes her off, as if she believes only time will ease Elly's awkwardness.

But it doesn't. At one point Elly is taking care of the children when she mysteriously disappears. The men are busy playing vollebyall, Sepideh and Shohreh are out shopping, and Naazy's cleaning indoors, when suddenly two of the children come rushing out to their fathers and demand help with Arash, the young son of Peyman and Shohreh.

The boy is seen floating in the water. The men begin to yell and dive in. Help soon arrives in the form of lifeguards, who save the young boy in a gripping, terrifying sequence.

Once Arash begins to breathe again, the adults look around: Who was watching the children? It's half curiosity and half accusation. Elly was. Where is she? Why didn't she see him?

Their panic rebounds when they realize Elly is missing. Her rescue mission is not successful. The authorities and more lifeguards become involved and send out a search and rescue unit, but to no avail. The horrified ensemble tries to wrap their minds about what has happened, their denial over her possible death leading them to all kinds of possibilities.

"I can't find her bag! Maybe she left?" Naazy exclaims after searching the house. This plants seeds of doubt into their heads as they try to reason why Elly would have left.

The camera flips from one character to the next as they compete to theorize how Elly is alive. It's their selfish resort to keep a small modicum of sanity—an abrupt and rude departure is surely not as bad as her death—but there is little to back up the idea.

Sepideh reveals the cupboard where she hid Elly's bag, in an attempt to deter from leaving.

The authorities have little sympathy for the crew when they find out that no one knows Elly's real first or last name. "Elham, Elnaz, Elmira . . . ? What's her full name?" Even Sepideh is clueless, immediately making her look more guilty. This is one of the most direct punches the film delivers. It seems to both reify the paranoia that is so systemic in Iranian society and bring into question whether it actually stems from blind privilege, the middle-class remaining so oblivious to the lower class they don't even bother to learn their names.

As the film progresses, more and more lies emerge and cloud Elly's existence in further mystery. Amir finds Elly's phone in Sepideh's purse, demanding why she would have been hiding it from the others. Manouchehr and Ahmad go to the neighboring villa where there is phone reception to contact Elly's family. But they encounter their own dilemma—Elly's mother doesn't pick up at first and when she does, she lies about Elly's location, even claiming the girl left her mobile at home.

The situation continues to grow in complexity and perplexity. Ahmad calls a number on Elly's phone, someone who turns out to be her brother. "I felt compelled to tell him the truth," he says to the group. "You told him she drowned?" Amir asks. "No, that she had an accident." For Ahmad, this white lie is the closest equivalent to the truth he could muster.

Ahmad and Sepideh return to town in order to meet up with Elly's brother Alireza, when Sepideh finally admits that the man must be Elly's fiancé, for she was an only child. Ahmad is in shock about what Sepideh has "done to them," but Sepideh claims her heart was in the right place. Elly had been trying to break things off with her fiancé for six months, and Sepideh saw an opportunity to fix Elly's unlucky love life.

This news is revelatory and damning for the group, pulling them into a full-on panic mode. Their reaction may seem exaggerated to Western audiences, but it's completely in sync with the Islamicate values in Iranian society. Women who are already engaged to a man are meant to be more protected by their family and are prevented from spending time with strangers, particularly men. Now the group has to explain to Elly's fiancé that she not only drowned, but that it happened while in the presence of strangers.

They all decide to claim ignorance—going along with Alireza's story that he's her brother—but he admits himself to the group, revealing that Elly frequently distances herself. The film intelligently ensures that every character in the film—even Alireza—is put into a position where lying is the more reasonable answer.

His discovery that the group were trying to find Elly a fiancé—from the housekeeper who asks about "the newlyweds"—hits him hard. The group's decision to lie to Alireza—they didn't know about her true marital status—is also an interesting cultural phenomenon in which paranoia causes groups to condone immoral behavior in order to save themselves. They again selfishly choose themselves over others, letting an innocent man believe his wife-to-be never informed her new friends about his existence and carried on with their shenanigans, pretending to be single. Their actions dishonor the dead Elly's dignity and warp Alireza's perception of Elly's love for him. Sepideh, the only one resistant to conducting this psychological abuse on an unwitting man, eventually conforms, not wanting to let down her group.

The film pairs the weight of the emotional horrors endured by its characters with a refined formal style. Its omission of musical cues in place of the roars of the sea turn it into a haunting riff that physically wears down the characters. "The sound of the sea drives me crazy!" an exasperated Shohreh tells her husband Peyman.

The disparate, isolating location of the tragedy—the beautiful calm Caspian Sea, which transforms into an inescapable prison of nature—is like a metaphor for Iranian society itself. Once a rarefied culture, its inhabitants have turned on each other.

## *A Separation*

*Divorce Iranian Style*

> At this time many Iranians all over the world are watching us and I imagine them to be very happy. They are happy not just because of an important award or a film or a filmmaker, but because at the time when talk of war, intimidation, and aggression is exchanged between politicians, the name of their country, Iran, is spoken here through her glorious culture, a rich and ancient culture that has been hidden under the heavy dust of politics. I proudly offer this award to the people of my country, the people who respect all cultures and civilizations and despise hostility and resentment. — Asghar Farhadi, at the 84th Academy Awards

*Nader and Simin request a divorce from the court, but their rationale is denied. She wants to leave the country, as their visas expire in a month, while he refuses to abandon his senile father (who suffers from Alzheimer's). The two, left at an impasse, decide it's best to separate. Their eleven-year-old daughter Termeh decides to stay with Dad, believing she can convince Mom to come back. Simin* moves in with her mother while Nader hires a caretaker for his ailing father. The hired help, Razieh, is a religious woman who so happens to be pregnant. She brings along her daughter Somayeh to work, and on the third day loses track of the father, who has ambled outside by a busy intersection. She crosses the street to retrieve him, and later on the bus ride home falls ill. The next day at work, she inexplicably leaves early and ties him to the bed. Nader and Termeh arrive to find the father badly bruised and mute, blaming Razieh's impulsive absence for his condition. When Nader finds money missing he becomes belligerent and suspicious, throwing her out of his apartment. She ends up injuring herself on the staircase and later suffers from a miscarriage. Her husband Hodjat blames Nader, and the two families take up the matter in court. Nader's informed that if he knew about her pregnancy, he can receive a 1-3 year prison sentence for manslaughter. He denies knowledge of Razieh's pregnancy—claiming her chador hid her pregnant belly—and Termeh's teacher even testifies on his behalf (she was present at their house and gave Razieh a recommendation for a gynocologist while Nader was in the kitchen). Later Termeh finds out her father did know, and the teacher withdraws her testimony after Nader unwittingly reveals his lie. Simin tries to mend matters by offering Razieh's family financial restitution—a much-needed offer on Hodjat's part, considering his lenders are after him—when Razieh drops another bomb: that she had been in a car accident the day before the miscarriage trying to safely fetch Nader's father on the street. She's uncertain whether that may have cost her her unborn child. Knowing Razieh is a devout woman whose doubt would prevent her from taking blood money, Nader asks her to swear his actions caused her miscarriage on the Koran. The film ends with Hodjat hitting himself as Razieh refuses to answer affirmatively, and Termeh being summoned in court to choose which parent she'd like to live with. The film closes ambiguously as the parents are asked to wait outside while she finalizes her decision.

---

*A Separation* is Asghar Farhadi's magnum opus, a *sui generis* in his oeuvre, Iranian cinema, and indeed within the larger history of cinema itself. The production catapulted the filmmaker to a high degree of mainstream international acclaim and affected the political tensions between Iran and the West at a time of high tension. Its significance as a globalizing cultural product that updated the world's blurry image of Iran should be neither underestimated nor forgotten.

"...*A Separation* is a fine account of Iran's predicament; anyone interested in the mysteries of change and tradition—the difficulties faced by many people as they try and reconcile themselves to modern values and norms—will learn much from it," wrote one anonymous writer for *The New York Review of Books*.[1]

The work continued Farhadi's examination of the plurality of moral perspectives within a society entangled between modernity and tradition. But here, formally and narratively, Farhadi reached an aesthetic zenith. Here, more distinctly and clearly than in his other films, Farhadi demonstrates the problematic dynamics separating different classes, genders and generations. The film never favors one character over another—the religiously devout Razieh and her hot-tempered husband Hodjat are as relatable as the ostensible protagonist of the film, Nader. It's fair to say that everyone in this film is prone to making mistakes—decisions they believe are right in the heat of the moment—and though the film begs us to judge them for it, we strangely find ourselves unable to do so.

Formally, Farhadi shows a colossal improvement between *About Elly* and *A Separation*. This is most apparent in narrative and visual style. Colors are muted and kept neutral on purpose (outside a few strands of bright red hair that dart out of Simin's headscarf). The camera captures its characters and environments with a hyperrealistic eye, crisply making out the most mundane of details in spite of the constricted contours of apartments, corridors, staircases and vehicles. This is all thanks to Mahmoud Kalari's stunning cinematography, which Farhadi had decided to collaborate on extensively in the months leading up to production. The two brainstormed ideas for the look and feel of the film, sharing notes on their favorite Iranian documentaries.[2] The handiwork has been (favorably) compared to Dogme 95, but combined with the kinetic, intuitive editing rhythm from Hayedeh Safiari, the end result is more dizzying and engrossing, planting viewers in the characters' most intimate moments while obscuring their figures just behind the claustrophobic reach of doorframes, windows and other interior infrastructure.

The "button" for this film's "suit" was an image of a middle-aged man washing his senile father in the bath and crying. Though Farhadi has never experienced this personally, his grandfather did suffer from Alzheimer's.

"I wanted to know: 'Who is this man? Where is his family? Why is he keeping his dad in the house? Why is he responsible for washing him? And does his father even recognize him?'" Farhadi told Roger Ebert. "And so many other questions. These really made different aspects of the story come to light for me."[3]

The level of story detail in *A Separation* is unparalleled for Farhadi, but what's most interesting about the film's narrative and thematic complexity is how the film remains completely open to interpretation. It's rich with subtext, even within the opening seconds of the credits sequence. Yes, even in those monotonous minutes as government documents are pressed against a photocopier, one can read between the lines.

The forms of identification shown in *A Separation* are static like the composition of the shot; the information they provide belongs to a governmental and legal system that is immutable, predefined, and basic, unlike the amorphous nature of the characters in the film. The printer makes copies of the documents as if cloning the individuals of the film, but their pictures and legal statuses remain identical. In the reality of the film, the characters change and each new "version" of themselves becomes a different person with new ideas and perspectives. For example, though Simin does not actually want to separate from Nader (despite claiming to), her opinion of him changes throughout the course of the film.

This credits sequence shows us the sanctified and tangible representation of the law, with its black-and-white parameters of the truth and its black-and-white photographs of citizens. The static nature of these legal documents provide a striking visual contradiction to what the film will eventually unearth on a thematic level. The film is ultimately an exploration about the murky phenomenon of determining the truth in legal matters, the nebulous nature of morality, and the multitude of opinions and ideas that can be simultaneously correct and just. The straightforward and austere presentation of these legal documents at the commencement of the film is an ironic presentation of the characters they represent.

The film moves from showing head shots of a married couple from another of Farhadi's films—Morteza and Mojdeh from *Fireworks Wednesday*, to be exact—to the real, flesh-and-blood faces of Nader and Simin. Within a medium-close-up frame, the two characters face the camera as if the viewer him- or herself is the judge. Evidently, this camera setup was deliberate: "We are also the judge. We will reach a verdict during the movie by following their story," claims Farhadi in the DVD audio commentary of the film.[4]

This equation of the viewer as judge may seem like a simple visual device, yet its execution is necessitated by the film's major thematic undertones, as noted by Adam Nayman: "The direct address of this opening puts us in the same position as the magistrate, presenting us with two people and their respective lines of reasoning, and begging our observation and observance, if not our outright judgment. This is an apt overture for a film that is explicitly about how slippery the onus of interpretation can be—especially when all parties involved would seem to have a pretty good case."[5]

It doesn't take long before the couple begins to argue. Equally brisk is the film's development of exposition, neatly using the pretense of their argument as a means to set up the primary catalyst of the film. Simin would like to leave the country with her family while they still have the chance (their visas expire in 40 days), while Nader refuses to leave behind his elderly father, who has Alzheimer's disease. Publicly and without hesitation, the two begin to row in front of the judge about their problem in such a frustrated and rehearsed manner that it can only be surmised the couple has conducted this exact same argument repeatedly over months, nary a compromise in sight. Though heated, their debate remains civil; the two clearly love and respect each other. When asked about her husband Simin responds, "On the contrary. He is a decent man." Unlike many breakups, this marital stalemate demonstrates the couple's extant love for one another, slightly eroded by their hardened positions and need for agency.

"... [T]he important thing is that both characters come across as decent ordinary people with equally compelling reasons for their positions," argued Godfrey Cheshire in *Film Comment*. "What woman wouldn't leap at the long-dreamed-of chance to leave Iran? What son would abandon his stricken father for the same opportunity? The film's emotional complexity begins with the fact that most viewers will be induced to sympathize deeply with both sides in this standoff."[6]

This faultless nature extends through to every decision every character makes—even the more morally dubious ones. Even their "gestures, manners, habits, turns of speech, turns of thoughts, styles of face" are "morally expressive," according to Joseph Burke,[7] and the intuitive, roaming eye of the handicam nimbly captures each and every detail. Beginning with this strong stalemate between Nader and Simin, the film boldly asserts its thesis about the complexity of moral relativism early on. There is nothing inherently wrong with Simin wanting to emigrate for the prosperity and future of her child; the same applies to Nader's devotion to his father. Within minutes, the film has challenged the viewer with a tangible Iranian experiment in utilitarianism. The viewer is asked to contemplate the situation as if it's their own: Should you jeopardize your child's future or disrespect the man who raised you by abandoning him in his final days? Do you settle for the just-barely-acceptable "circumstances" in Islamic Iran, in order to take care of a man who doesn't even recognize his own son? Who is more important—Termeh, their 11-year-old daughter, or Nader's elderly father? To put it symbolically: what is more important—the past or the future?

There is no correct answer to these questions; even if viewers are wont to subconsciously choose a side. Western viewers, for example, may be more tempted to side with Simin because they may project onto Iran an image of its living conditions as being impoverished and a miserable place for youth, particularly women. Yet ultimately, even with such biases, the viewer will find it impossible not to sympathize on some deep level with the other side.

Nader and Simin clearly love and respect each other, and the bitterness each feels about their predicament is visible within this scene alone. It has changed their relationship, and the rest of the film cements each of their positions on the matter.

Though Nader and Simin's arguments are warranted and stem from personal, ideological reasons, the judge is unwilling to grant them a divorce and tells them to stop wasting the court's time. Without the legal permission to divorce, the couple decides to separate, with Simin moving in with her mother and trying unsuccessfully to take Termeh with her. Throughout the film, the couple's relationship becomes complicated and changed by a succession of outside events that ultimately determine whether or not they will get back together.

Nader must hire a full-time caretaker for his dad after Simin moves out, because he works full-time as a bank manager and Termeh is in school. An acquaintance of Simin's recommends her sister-in-law, Razieh, (Sareh Bayat), whom Nader ultimately hires.

A pivotal scene is the one in which Simin packs her belongings while Nadir instructs Razieh how to take care of his dad. Little happens in this scene, but the stressful atmosphere is imperative to establish the broken-down dynamic of the family and how Simin doesn't want to leave. She moves around quickly but inefficiently, spying on her two family members and trying to come up with reasons not to leave. She takes money out of a drawer, irritably inquires about the location of a Mohammad Reza Shajarian CD that she'd like to take with her, and finally gets out of the house.

The subsequent scenes of Razieh and her young child Somayeh work out certain kinks in the work arrangement, but they also serve to complicate the nature of her employment. When Nader's father soils himself, the frazzled Razieh must call her local imam to check whether or not it's sinful to change the man. She tells Nader she can't take the job, giving Nader his first pause with Razieh's behavior. When she explains, he's mortified but also in disbelief. Razieh's solution—that her husband do the work instead—is sufficient for Nader, but the next day she's obliged to return when her husband goes face-to-face with hounding creditors.

The next few scenes, in terms of what they show and, more importantly, what they leave out, prove to be critical in our understanding of the narrative events that implode shortly thereafter. We see Razieh leaving the apartment to go after Nader's father, who has gone astray outdoors, and we see her impatiently waiting to cross the street. A jolting cut to a foosball table where Nader, Termeh, Somayeh, and even Nader's father are rambunctiously playing is subtly juxtaposed with a shot of an ill-looking Razieh slowly washing her face. On the third day, Nazer and Termeh arrive home to find Grandfather toppled by his bed, nearly unconscious. He'd been tied to the foot of the bed and had fallen over. When Razieh arrives back from some urgent appointment—she never gets a chance to explain, and Nader is quick to dismiss its importance—he becomes belligerent and suspicious of her work ethic, literally throwing her out of the apartment.

We never see the force of his push because the camera remains on the inside of the apartment unit, but suddenly there's a fall, Somayeh is crying, and neighbors are rushing out to help. Nader looks out and we glimpse on his face a brief expression of guilt, but it passes.

Until, of course, he finds out she's miscarried her baby.

From here, the reintroduction of Simin and Hodjat into the story as the two families begin an unflinching war about Nader's complicity in the baby's death further complicates and deepens the narrative with such intricate articulation it truly boggles the viewer's mind (even upon repeated screenings). Did Nader know Razieh was pregnant? This becomes a crucial piece of information, for his knowledge equals a murder charge. And though he claims not to have known—and for all intents and purposes, seems to be telling the truth—it turns out the "truth" is much more complicated. "Look, I knew she was pregnant, but I didn't know at that moment. I had forgotten. I wasn't paying attention," he later explains to Termeh when she finds him out.

The film is very emphatic about the ways in which deception is taught to Iran's younger generations. Nader is particularly keen on teaching Termeh the "right" way to do things: choose the correct, Persian word over the Arabic word in dictation, even if the teacher docks you marks. If you forget to ask for change from the gas attendant, it's perfectly acceptable to go back and ask for it—and you should. Nader believes in defending his honor and tries to dissuade Termeh from becoming like her mother, a woman whose flexibility in arrangements and understandings of what is so-deemed "right" changes based on the circumstances (as Farhadi has frequently explained about the binary dividing Nader and Simin, he belongs to a traditionalist past and she to a modern future). Nader's lie is yet another moral lesson for Termeh: sometimes it's okay to lie, because in this society, in this legal system, you have no other choice.

Without a clear system allowing Termeh to decide what to do, she can become lost. The film isn't trying to compare this unfavorably to Razieh's religious approach—her doubt near the end of the film, which causes her to refuse the money from Nader and Simin, is problematic for its own reasons—but simply to demonstrate that no matter what philosophy or theology or ideology one maintains, there will always remain good and bad consequences from our decisions.

The film demonstrates the subtle and not-so-subtle gestures the upper-middle-class take to dismiss and ridicule those below them. As Javad Toossi astutely points out in *Film Monthly*, the scene in which Nader calmly tells the driver behind to wait is a sign of the collected demeanor the Iranian middle class have subconsciously affected. Their logical calm in dealing with the harangued society in what is deemed to be the better way predisposes them to a superior position (in their eyes, at least). "Nader has now become so experienced in the social progression between the classes that he can manipulate the weaknesses of those beneath him, and at the same time maintain his image of self-righteousness and being reasonable."[8]

This maneuvering extends to the final scene, in which Nader slyly asks

Razieh to swear on the Koran that he caused her miscarriage instead of her car accident. He knows she can't.

As Michael Sicinski has pointed out, it's exactly this level of permeability the film demonstrates that allows viewers—even Iranian clerics—to find their own interpretations and scapegoats in the film. "I suppose the cine-mullahs of the Islamic Republic . . . see a validation of humble values, an indictment of the exploitation of poor, unsophisticated Shia traditionalists by the decadent bourgeoisie."[9]

The film's domestic reception oscillated between national pride and utter contempt. The year before *A Separation* premiered, Farhadi's public remarks supporting dissident filmmakers Mohsen Makhmalbaf and Jafar Panahi were taken seriously by the government and officials delayed the film's production. After revoking his comments and issuing an apology—Farhadi claimed he had been misinterpreted—the government lifted the ban on his film.[10] The domestic release was as successful as its international reception, and Iran submitted *A Separation* as its best foreign language film contender for the 84th Academy Awards, which it won—the first Iranian film to do so, sixteen years after *The White Balloon* had received Iran's sole other nomination. The film was also nominated for best screenplay at the Oscars, and garnered a whopping 79 awards and 26 other nominations after its international releases. The film was the first to win three Bears at Berlinale and the first Iranian film to win a Golden Globe.[11] The film was a huge commercial success for Farhadi—the most profitable Iranian film in history—amassing 20 million dollars worldwide.[12] *A Separation* appeared on numerous year-end critics polls, with many—including Roger Ebert—naming it "the best film of 2011."[13]

It was the first Iranian film to have such a wide-ranging and resounding cultural impact on the image of Iran, and though Farhadi resisted descriptions that *A Separation* was some kind of complete cross-section of Iranian society—a film-cum-encyclopedia that could teach people about how everything works in the country—he inversely did become a cultural ambassador of sorts, a move he politicized in both his Golden Globe and Oscars speeches, sincerely describing his people "who respect all cultures and civilizations and despise hostility and resentment." It's easy to describe Farhadi as a secularist whose disdain for the Iranian government is perfectly shielded—his speeches and several interview responses differentiate between his fellow citizens and the government on purpose—yet even though his beliefs creep in from time to time (and in some cases, have forced him to retract his comments), one can barely blame an artist for being forced to walk on such an unwieldly tightrope.

## The Past

*An Iranian in Paris*

*Ahmad meets his ex-wife Marie at the airport. Having arrived in Paris from Tehran to finalize their divorce, the two fall into a familiar cycle of old routines and arguments that is coupled by the awkwardness of their situation. Ahmad is dismayed that Marie didn't book him a hotel, while Marie claims she wasn't sure he would show up. He reluctantly agrees to stay at her place, but she omits telling him about her new partner and fiancé, Samir, and his child Fouad, who live with her. Ahmad begins to piece things together when he encounters Fouad playing in the yard with Lea, the girl whom Ahmad had raised as a stepdaughter. She delights in her recognition of him and soon Ahmad feels himself falling back into his familiar role as parent, husband, handyman, and mediator. Drawn into the melodrama that is Marie's family life, he finds himself fixing Lea's bike, cleaning up paint, fixing a pipe, making an elaborate meal, and playing surrogate dad to all the children. Marie doesn't ask for anything nor does she mind his help. One thing she does request is that Ahmad talk to her adolescent daughter Lucie (who trusts Ahmad more than her own mother), as she dislikes Samir for no apparent reason, and is vehemently opposed to their engagement. Lucie slowly unravels the horrible truth about Samir and Marie's relationship: Samir's wife Celine is in a coma as a result of having found out about their affair. Lucie doesn't just*

despise Samir and Marie for what they did to a depressed woman, though. She also blames herself for forwarding their love-letter emails to Celine, which she'd done the day before Celine killed herself. Marie and Lucie's relationship reaches new lows when she runs away and hides at the house of Ahmad's friend. Ahmad and Marie begin to argue about her daughter as if they were still together, raising Samir's ire. Ahmad finds himself both detesting his involvement and incapable of abandoning the vulnerable teenager in her time of need. Lucie is finally pushed to tell Ahmad this truth when Samir asks his employee, Naima, to convince them that Celine's suicide was prompted by her depression and a nasty incident with a client at Samir's dry-cleaning business. Ahmad convinces Lucie to tell her mother the truth, claiming that it will clear the air. He finds it crucial that Marie know the truth because she's pregnant with Samir's baby (a truth Marie also takes her time unloading to both Ahmad and Lucie). Trusting Ahmad's judgment, Lucie does as asked, but the effect is painfully explosive: Marie erupts in anger, pushing Lucie away. When the two calm down and begin to accept the reality of what's happened, Marie contemplates telling Samir. Lucie tells her she must. But when Marie tries to gently break the news to her fiancé, Samir remains in denial, doubting Lucie's actions. This is based on the fact that Celine wasn't at the drycleaner the day before her suicide. He finally deduces that when Lucie called his store, she talked to Naima, who pretended to be his wife. Naima—who Celine suspected was sleeping with Samir—believes Lucie's forwarded emails could finally redeem Naima in Celine's eyes. Samir is so angry at what Naima's done—having inadvertently caused Celine's comatose state—that he immediately fires her. Several questions remain about Celine's suicide, and without her conscious state of mind to answer them, the other characters stew in their anger, resentment, and guilt. Why did Celine kill herself while she was pregnant with Samir's child? Why did she drink laundry detergent in front of Naima instead of Samir or Marie? The film ends on more than one ambiguous note. Informed by Celine's doctors that a familiar scent may be the key to waking her, Samir takes several perfumes to her hospital bed and gingerly tries one on. A tear rolls down Celine's face as Samir asks her to squeeze his finger, enclosing his hand in hers. Their hands remain steady.

---

*The Past* was Asghar Farhadi's first film made outside of his home country, a production that reconfirmed his position in the international film scene. Though *A Separation* made a bigger splash, *The Past*, a collaboration with European producers, crew, and a big-name cast, was a sign that the filmmaker was ready and capable to work outside of his comfort zone. The film also affirmed that, despite the cultural specificity of his previous work, Farhadi could adapt his dramatist style for any setting—even a city that had been represented in cinema countless times: Paris, France.

The production of the film was a bit of a challenge for the filmmaker, who was used to working in his native tongue. Having an interpreter onset was necessary for him to communicate clearly with his crew and especially his cast, with whom he worked for months in rehearsals and whose lines were almost entirely in French. Furthermore, the production scale was larger (more crew members, a bigger budget) and Farhadi had to navigate a foreign production system. Despite the cultural barriers, Farhadi says he welcomed the challenge.

"There are several aspects to language: there's the music of it, the information that is imparted through it, and the cultural roots of a nation," he said in an interview for *HitFix*. "Very often, we may know another language but are incapable of penetrating its culture and identity. I was in France for two years, so on numerous days I walked the streets and listened to people talk to each other. I didn't understand much but I did try to absorb the melody and music of it."[1]

Farhadi came up with the basic premise of *The Past* several years prior, when a friend confided that he had to travel to another country for a few days to finalize his divorce with his ex-wife.

"And that thought never really left my mind: how strange it must be to have been apart from a woman all that time, and then spend several days with her to say goodbye," he explained in the same interview.[2]

Pre-production plans with partners in France and Italy were already in the works by the time Farhadi was on the road screening *A Separation* internationally. Though the majority of *The Past*'s cast and crew were French, Farhadi did bring with him an Iranian contingent. First he cast two well-known Iranian actors: Ali Mosaffa as Ahmad and Babak Karimi as Ahmad's friend, Shahryar (he also appears briefly as the court interrogator in *A Separation*). Mahmoud Kalari returned as Farhadi's cinematographer, but for the first time in years Farhadi hired a different editor (Juliette Welfling) instead of Hayedeh Safiyari, who had worked with him on his three previous films.

Several other crew members were also Iranian, including head of sound (Dana Farzanehpour) and some assistant directors (Nogole Khodabandeh, Maryam Naraghi, Nassime Nazari, and Farhad Taghizadeh Toussi).

These crew members are important to point out because of the slight controversy that erupted in Iran when the film was chosen as the country's official submission for best foreign-language film at the 86th Academy Awards.

Some critical of the decision argued that the film's producers were European, its dialogue and setting were French, and many of its cast and crew were non-Iranian. But Farhadi argued that not only did the film employ a fair number of Iranians, it also had an "Iranian gaze."[3]

What makes the film "Iranian"—more so than any other factor—is that Farhadi was at the helm of the production. Inside and out of Iran, he is seen as an ambassador for his country and he brought to *The Past* a sensibility that cannot in any way be described as European, no matter who's funding the film. From an auteurist perspective, that alone guides the cultural identity of a film. Like Abbas Kiarostami and others before him, Farhadi is expanding the definition and notion of Iranian cinema. In this film particularly, Farhadi has keyed into an important phenomenon that concerns Iranian identity: the diasporic experience that millions of Iranians have encountered upon leaving their country.[4]

In our interview, Farhadi commented on how having the blend of cultures during the production was occasionally a strange but ultimately fruitful endeavour, with crew members learning from each other: "When I went to work in France, I knew that the French people who had joined my team had worked in France many times before and they had actually joined to see how Iranians work. They didn't want me to work like the French. They wanted to learn my style. The actors especially wanted to come to the set to see how I rehearse with my actors because it's not normal in Europe to train with the actors for so many months like theater."[5]

The film was nominated for a slew of awards (from the Palme d'Or to a Golden Globe for best foreign-language film), but only won a handful, among them Bérénice Bejo's Best Actress Award and Farhadi's Prize of the Ecumenical Jury at Cannes.[6]

Reception for the film matched the awards: though reviews were mostly positive, several critics strongly disliked the film or had mixed feelings. There was some consensus on whether or not Farhadi had successfully adapted his style in France, with most reviews falling on the positive end of the critical spectrum.

"*The Past* is a film that announces this director's arrival in the rank of those film-makers like Kiarostami, Haneke and PT Anderson, directors who are intent on the unfashionable business of making morally serious films for adults," wrote Peter Bradshaw for *The Guardian*. "Very often, a certain type of movie is praised for being 'immersive', for providing the longed-for sensual pleasure of pure cinema. Farhadi's kind of film is quite different, but just as valuable. You are not immersed; on the contrary, you are challenged, alienated, compelled to pay fierce attention to every line, every cutaway, every scene change, and then to question what you think you have learned."[7]

Commenting on how *The Past* proves Farhadi can work with movie stars, Mike D'Angelo notes that Farhadi's creative move to France could be interpreted as a response to *A Separation*'s reception:

"This, perhaps, is in response to foreigners who downplayed *A Separation*'s heartbreaking, universal themes to insist on its cultural specificity. (They weren't wrong, necessarily; they just misplaced the emphasis.) The result demonstrates that Farhadi, who is cinema's heir to the likes of Henrik Ibsen and Anton Chekhov, is so deft at ingenious narrative construction and intricate character development that he can make first-rate dramas in any country and/or language he likes."[8]

Farhadi did believe that following the success of *A Separation*, too many critics mistakenly called the film a comprehensive cross-section of how Iranian society operates. One of the great accomplishments of that film is how it both ties into specific cultural details and still manages to consistently maintain a universal essence that appeals to cinephiles the world over. With *The Past*, Farhadi brings an Iranian element into a French setting, and though the script ensures a degree of obvious cultural markers—Ahmad's way of teaching Marie's (Bérénice Bejo) young daughters Farsi and his making of a traditional meal, *ghormeh sabzi*—the experience of the diaspora is relatable to anyone who's moved abroad, Iranian or not.

That experience extends to other characters in the film and it manifests in a variety of different directions, though their thematic implications are occasionally muddled and unclear. "*The Past*" is as much a reference to the events that led to Céline being in a coma (or Ahmad's breakdown and breakup with Marie) as it is about the experience of immigration and the abandonment of one's native culture. The film never specifies the ethnicities of Samir (Tahar Rahim) or Naïma (Sabrina Ouazani), but they are both clearly Arab (Samir likely second-generation, based on his accent), and there is a sense that Samir's decision to hire an illegal worker for his business was a sympathetic gesture, from someone who understands what it's like to arrive alone and penniless in a foreign country. While Ahmad's own identity was too entrenched for him to stick around in Paris after breaking up with Marie (thus forcing him back to Iran), Samir is caught up in his own past—not a cultural one, but a more deeply psychological memory of what it was like when his wife was still alive. Then there's Naïma, a serviceable and cordial, albeit highly anxious, woman who is afraid of being found out by the police for her illegal work status. In contrast to Ahmad, the younger Naïma is trying hard to make it work in her new country. Unfortunately, she ultimately botches things when she becomes involved in the psychologically unsound affairs of Samir's love life.

Ahmad's trip back to France, though a sensible decision in some respects—he explains to a suspicious Samir that he needed to be present with Marie's family in order to bring closure—is also proof that something is amiss for him in Iran. Four years later, he's still an incomplete individual and finds reasons to stay (indeed, he makes the unusual decision to not book a roundtrip flight, putting off his departure until he's good and ready to leave). When Marie insists that Ahmad speak to Lucie about her issues, he sees a paternal obligation to stay behind and patch things up between all the family members (this despite not being Lucie's biological father). His need to play psychologist in a fixer-upper family (with a house to match) demonstrates that on some level, he's having a hard time putting his own past behind him. And the film is not shy to point that out, and does so in the form of his Iranian friend Shahryar, who tells him matter-of-factly that Ahmad cannot remain in this liminal state. He must choose: Paris or Iran.

"*The Past* can perhaps be seen as a film about a crisis of permeability, of insufficient boundaries between timeframes," argues Michael Sicinski in his positive review. "If *A Separation* is about firm lines and portals, and what happens which you let someone who 'doesn't belong' enter your threshold, *The Past* details the dangers of ragged endings, things that cling and hang on, people as ghosts and vestigial appendages."[9]

The visuals in *The Past* support this thesis (Ahmad is as much a ghost as Marie's house is haunted, with its half-painted doors and shadowy, dilapidated features), but the cinematic language doesn't seem to demonstrate any kind of aesthetic progression from *A Separation* (this is not necessarily a negative unto itself, as one could claim the filmmaker has reached a zenith of sorts as far as this particular vein of filmmaking is concerned). There are a few interesting compositions, such as the perspective of a panning camera (clearly Ahmad's) as he enters Marie's run-down house for the first time, glancing through the bushy gates that lead to a dilapidated yard full of childhood trinkets and toys, as if he were an intruder. And like in almost every single Farhadi film, windows are used for purposes of surveillance, as the grownups watch each other interact with the children.

The film nonetheless suffers from aesthetic contrivances that are disappointingly pressing and glaring. Ahmad is an easy-enough character to interpret and read into. He's a well-fleshed-out protagonist (and unsurprisingly, the only Iranian one) but the film's treatment of Marie leaves something to be desired. The film is diligent in transferring the perspective from one character to another so that no one can be deemed a villain. This is shown elegantly with Samir and Fouad's characters, who are initially portrayed as sullen, cranky father and son. But Marie's character is positioned in such a way that she comes off as an unstable mother who makes one bad life decision after another. She divorces and marries multiple times, smokes while pregnant, carries on an affair with a married man, and emotionally abuses her fiancé's child and her own daughters. Despite Bejo's phenomenal performance, *The Past* doesn't give us as many glimpses into her character or her past, other than outlining the fact that she drives everyone crazy (at least three different characters utter this statement at some point in the film).

The film's themes feel less resonant than Farhadi's previous output, perhaps because there is little societal grounding that can provide rich subtext. This may be because Farhadi had to imagine his own past inside a foreign city, but though he tried to immerse himself in the atmosphere of French culture for two years while writing the script, the only true accomplishment is that the film feels realistic insofar as that it *could* have happened in France. Or elsewhere, for that matter. According to Farhadi, he chose Paris because the city's rich history matches the film's preoccupation with the past,[10] but this connection barely registers as an idea, visually. Though most of the film takes place inside Marie's rotting house, there are multiple scenes shot in cosmopolitan streets that seem intended, more than anything, to anonymize the locale. One could say it's a refreshingly unromantic look at Paris that is at odds with most representations of the city in the history of cinema, but that's missing the point for a Farhadi film, given that so much of his work is situated in physical spaces that feel very much rooted in reality (for example, the *Shahnameh* statue in *Dancing in the Dust*, and the juvenile penitentiary and the poverty-stricken neighborhood by the railroad in *Beautiful City*).

Without the infrastructure of culture and society to sustain the ideas and themes pertinent to the film, the screenplay's faults seem that much more conspicuous. Though the film seems thoughtfully plotted and reenacted—with crisp visuals, pitch-perfect performances from the entire cast, and a kind of cinematic dexterity that demonstrates Farhadi's stature as not only a great screenwriter but a bona-fide master director and even, yes, an auteur—one of his greatest attributes as an artist is his acuity as a storyteller. *A Separation* may have been the peak of that talent, but *The Past* demonstrates that even the Farhadi touch can be prone to contrivances.

Because so much of *The Past* is built on a mystery—whether or not Céline was aware of Samir and Marie's affair when she killed herself—it is altogether strange that the film takes more than half of its already-long running time to establish this unanswerable question as the film's central hypothesis. While Farhadi has never shied away from following atypical narrative structures—it takes over 40 minutes before the central event in *About Elly* occurs—*The Past* lacks *About Elly*'s grace and enchantment (the *ghormeh sabzi* scene is one exception, but notice that once again the film's strength is a scene in which a character gets to celebrate Iranian culture). Virtually every conversation leads to an argument or a standoff; every interaction is charged with tension and a kind of negativity that grows quickly arduous.

The first half of the film also squanders its opportunities to fill in some of the more trivial details about the characters—such as Ahmad's relationship to Marie's children—forcing the viewer to play an exhausting game of detective before the main mystery has even presented itself.

The use of the emails Lucie allegedly sent to Céline—and their effect on her mental state—become a belabored device near the end of the film after one too many turns from characters full of doubt. When Samir can't believe that Lucie could have sent his wife the emails, he double-checks with Naïma about the timing, which conflicts with Lucie's account. Ultimately, it's revealed in yet another twist that Naïma was the one to blame, as she pretended to be his wife for her own ulterior motive. These kinds of eleventh-hour revelations don't particularly reward Samir's curiosity or that of the viewer, and by leaving it still ambiguous—the question remains as to why Céline would so boldly kill herself in front of Naïma instead of Marie or Samir if she'd known about their affair—the dramatic purposes of the entire story become fuzzy flecks of ambiguity instead of causing a viewer to contemplate the possible answer long after the film is done. This was the effect achieved with *A Separation*'s ambiguous ending regarding Termeh's decision about which parent to live with, and the same applies to the ending of *Beautiful City*, where more than one narrative thread is purposely left unresolved.

But *The Past* does temper the dysfunctionality of the ambiguous-ending device with its closing scene. The final question—also left unresolved—becomes whether or not Céline will survive and wake out of her coma. With Samir's attempt to arouse his near-dead wife by using her favorite scents, the film suggests that the answer is, on some level, irrelevant. Like Marie's unresolved feelings for Ahmad, Samir feels much more conflicted about the situation he's caused with Céline and Marie. This last scene is beautifully captured, from Samir's pause in the hallway (instigating his decision to go back and re-try the perfumes after the nurse tells him they didn't work) to the way his hand holds Céline's as the film ends on its tragic note and the credits begin to appear. This scene is charged with the anticipation of her waking up, but despite the tension, the scene remains elegantly austere in its composition and blocking. Samir puts on his own cologne—her favorite—and inches closer to Céline's comatose body so the scent can properly reach her nose. A tear rolls suddenly down her cheek. Is it just a benign physical reflex, so common in comatose patients, or does it signify an emotional and cognitive reaction from Céline? He barely notices, and asks her to squeeze his hand if she can hear him. The camera pans down towards their hands and as viewers we wait as eagerly as Samir, watching her hand like a hawk just in case a single muscle flexes. That's when the melancholic music and credits begin, but we stay with this image for a long time. What's beautiful about this ending, despite the film's many flaws, is not whether or not Céline wakes up. It's Samir's inability to let go of her hand, to let go of his past. In the film's final seconds, for one moment, the film's thesis finally registers. He can never forget her.

# Notes

## Introduction

1 Burke, Joseph, "Rediscovering Morality Through Asghar Farhadi's *A Separation*," *Senses of Cinema*, 2011, http://sensesofcinema.com/2011/feature-articles/rediscovering-morality-through-ashgar-farhadi%E2%80%99s-a-separation/.

2 Dabashi, Hamid, "The Tragic Endings of Iranian Cinema," *Aljazeera*, 2013, http://www.aljazeera.com/indepth/opinion/2013/03/2013320175739100357.html.

3 The discourse around arthouse films has been a long and exhausting debate in Iran, politicized and polemicized by government officials, critics, Iranians, and filmmakers alike. Hamid Naficy offers a comprehensive and fascinating account of this subject in *A Social History of Iranian Cinema*, Vol. 4, 251-261.

4 Cheshire, Godfrey, "*A Separation*: Scenes from a Marriage," *Film Comment*, 2012, http://www.filmcomment.com/article/scenes-from-a-marriage.

5 No author listed. "Asghar Farhadi's Iran," *Film Society of Lincoln Center*, http://www.filmlinc.com/films/series/asghar-farhadis-iran.

6 No author listed. "Tribeca '09 Interview: *About Elly* Director Asghar Farhadi," World Narrative Feature Competition, *Indiewire*, http://www.indiewire.com/article/tribeca_09_interview_about_elly_director_asghar_farhadi_world_narrative_fea.

7 Mehrabi, Masoud, "Bitter Truth, Sweet Compromise, and Deprived Redemption," *Film Monthly*, March 2011, Issue 424, 68-109.

**8** Sicinski, Michael, "*A Separation* (Asghar Farhadi, Iran)," *Cinema Scope* 49, 2011, http://cinema-scope.com/currency/currency-a-separation-asghar-farhadi-iran/.

**9** Burke, Joseph, "Rediscovering Morality Through Asghar Farhadi's *A Separation*," *Senses of Cinema*, 2011, http://sensesofcinema.com/2011/feature-articles/rediscovering-morality-through-ashgar-farhadi%E2%80%99s-a-separation/.

## Interview

**1** No author listed. "Asghar Farhadi, Oscar-Winning Iranian Director of *A Separation*, Says Next Film Will Be About PM Mohammad Mossadegh," *Melliun*, May 6, 2014, http://melliun.org/iran/40587.

**2** Smith, Damon, "Asghar Farhadi, *A Separatio*n," *Filmmaker Magazine*, 2011, http://filmmakermagazine.com/36713-asghar-farhadi-a-separation/.

**3** Short for *Kanoon-e Parvaresh-e Fekri-e Koodakan va Nojavanan* (Institute for the Intellectual Development of Children and Young Adults), a cultural institution founded by Empress Farah in the early 1960s. For more information on Kanun, please see Hamid Naficy's *A Social History of Iranian Cinema*, Vol. 2, 330.

**4** Rastin, Shadmehr, " 'Which part of this city is beautiful?'," *Film Monthly*, June 2004, Issue 318, 42-58.

**5** No author listed, "A half billion toman offer to an actress: Doubts about the financial future of filmmaking in Iran," *Tabnak*, July 22, 2014, http://www.tabnak.ir/fa/news/418467/.

**6** Marsh, Calum, " 'I Don't Really Believe in Endings': An Interview with Iranian Director Asghar Farhadi," *Hazlitt*, 2014, http://www.randomhouse.ca/hazlitt/feature/i-dont-really-believe-endings-interview-iranian-director-asghar-farhadi.

7 Rastin, Shadmehr, " 'Which part of this city is beautiful?,'" *Film Monthly*, June 2004, Issue 318, 42-58.

8 Mehrabi, Masoud, "Bitter Truth, Sweet Compromise, and Deprived Redemption," *Film Monthly*, March 2011, Issue 424, 68-109.

### Dancing in the Dust

1 Farhadi, Asghar, Personal Interview (Part One), T. Hassannia, June 14, 2014.

2 Rastin, Shadmehr, " 'Which part of this city is beautiful?,'" *Film Monthly*, June 2004, Issue 318, 42-58.

3 Farhadi, Asghar, Personal Interview (Part One), T. Hassannia, June 14, 2014.

4 The visual of the government IDs also underscores how heavily institutionalized the idea of love is in Iranian society, and is reminiscent of the photocopier scanning marriage certificates in *A Separation*.

### Beautiful City

1 Rastin, Shadmehr, " 'Which part of this city is beautiful?,'" *Film Monthly*, June 2004, Issue 318, 42-58.

2 Ibid.

3 Ibid.

4 No author listed. *"Beautiful City* (2004)—Awards," accessed July 1, 2014, http://www.imdb.com/title/tt0424434/awards?ref_=tt_ql_4.

5 Scheib, Ronnie, "Review: *Beautiful City*," *Variety*, 2004, http://variety.com/2004/film/reviews/beautiful-city-1200530703/.

6 Gonzalez, Ed, *"Beautiful City,"* *Slant Magazine*, 2006, http://www.slantmagazine.com/film/review/beautiful-city.

7 Kern, Laura, "A Plea For Forgiveness Sweetens Intricate Twists And Turns of Justice in Iran," *The New York Times*, 2006, http://www.nytimes.com/2006/03/15/movies/15beau.html.

8 For more information on the concept of *qesas* in the Koran and its implementation in Iran, see Saïd Amir Arjomand and Nathan J. Brown, *The Rule of Law, Islam, and Constitutional Politics in Egypt and Iran* (SUNY Press: 2013).

9 Blomfield, Bridget, "Fatimah," *Islamic Images and Ideas: Essays on Sacred Symbolism* (J. A. Morrow, McFarland & Company: 2013).

### Fireworks Wednesday

1 Oleinik, Anton, "Dostoevsky's Journey to Iran," *CineAction* 90, 2013, http://www.questia.com/read/1G1-332396180.

2 Farhadi, Asghar, Personal Interview (Part One), T. Hassannia, June 14, 2014.

3 Farhadi, Asghar, Personal Interview (Part One), T. Hassannia, June 14, 2014.

4 Price, Massoume, *Iran's Diverse Peoples: A Reference Sourcebook* (ABC-CLIO: 2005).

5 No author listed. "*Fireworks Wednesday* (2006)—Awards," accessed May 1, 2014, http://www.imdb.com/title/tt0845439/awards.

6 Young, Deborah, "Review: *Fireworks Wednesday*," *Variety*, 2006, http://variety.com/2006/film/reviews/fireworks-wednesday-1200518706/

7 Bradshaw, Peter, "*Fireworks Wednesday*—Review," *The Guardian*, 2014, http://www.theguardian.com/film/2014/feb/06/fireworks-wednesday-review.

**8** This scene is a more sophisticated version of one in *Dancing in the Dust*, in which two men fight outside a van, cracking its windshield.

**9** The staging of this sequence recalls the violent scene in Abbas Kiarostami's *The Report*, which similarly features a marriage on the verge of breakdown. When the protagonist beats his wife, the camera remains fixed outside the bedroom, but this does little to temper the shocking nature of the violence, as sounds (the cold, startling slaps, the shrieks of the woman, and the wailing of their child) form a sufficiently harrowing picture.

**10** Tizro, Zahra, *Domestic Violence in Iran: Women, Marriage, and Islam* (Routledge: 2013).

**11** O'Malley, Sheila, "…and Wednesday too: Asghar Farhadi's *Fireworks Wednesday*," *Slant Magazine*, 2007, http://www.slantmagazine.com/house/2007/30/and-wednesday-too-asghar-farhadis-fireworks-wednesday.

## *About Elly*

**1** Gamble, Patrick, "Film Review: *About Elly*," 2012, accessed July 19, 2014, http://www.cine-vue.com/2012/09/film-review-about-elly.html.

**2** Concannon, Phil, "*About Elly*—Review," *Little White Lies*, 2012, http://www.littlewhitelies.co.uk/theatrical-reviews/about-elly-21838.

**3** Hinrichsen, Jens, "Elly … ," *Film-Dienst* 1, 2011, 29-30.

**4** No author listed. "Director Blames Media for Playing Up Movie Censorship in Iran," *Deutsche Welle*, 2009, http://www.dw.de/director-blames-media-for-playing-up-movie-censorship-in-iran/a-4010651.

**5** No author listed. "*About Elly* (2009)—Awards," 2014, http://www.imdb.com/title/tt1360860/awards.

**6** Simon, Alissa, "Review: *About Elly*," *Variety*, 2009, http://variety.com/2009/film/reviews/about-elly-1200473803/.

7 Jahed, Parviz, "Film of the Year: *About Elly*," *Directory of World Cinema: Iran*, 2012. P. Jahed, *Intellect* 10, 11-13.

8 Kasman, Daniel, "Tribeca 2009: *About Elly* (Farhadi, Iran)," MUBI Notebook, 2009, https://mubi.com/notebook/posts/tribeca-2009-about-elly-farhadi-iran.

9 Kemp, Philip, "Film of the Week: *About Elly*," *Sight & Sound*, http://www.bfi.org.uk/news-opinion/sight-sound-magazine/reviews-recommendations/film-week-about-elly.

10 Jahed, Parviz, "Film of the Year: *About Elly*," *Directory of World Cinema: Iran*, 2012. P. Jahed, *Intellect* 10, 11-13.

11 Concannon, Phil, "About Elly—Review," *Little White Lies*, 2012, http://www.littlewhitelies.co.uk/theatrical-reviews/about-elly-21838.

## *A Separation*

1 Anonymous, "Tattered Lives in Divided Iran," *New York Review of Books*, 2011, http://www.nybooks.com/blogs/nyrblog/2011/sep/22/tattered-lives-divided-iran/.

2 Mehrabi, Masoud, "Bitter Truth, Sweet Compromise, and Deprived Redemption," *Film Monthly*, March 2011, Issue 424, 68-109.

3 Ebert, Roger, "Good People Facing Impossible Questions," *RogerEbert.com*, 2011, http://www.rogerebert.com/interviews/good-people-facing-impossible-questions.

4 No author listed. "Feature: Director's Commentary." *A Separation*, 2012, Sony Pictures Classic.

5 Nayman, Adam, "*A Separation*: Write Angles," *Reverse Shot*, 2011, http://www.reverseshot.com/article/separation.

6 Cheshire, Godfrey, "*A Separation*: Scenes from a Marriage," *Film Comment*, 2012, http://www.filmcomment.com/article/scenes-from-a-marriage.

**7** Burke, Joseph, "Rediscovering Morality Through Asghar Farhadi's *A Separation*," *Senses of Cinema*, 2011, http://sensesofcinema.com/2011/feature-articles/rediscovering-morality-through-ashgar-farhadi%E2%80%99s-a-separation/.

**8** Toossi, Javad, " 'Look at my tearful eyes,' " *Film Monthly*, March 2011, Issue 424, 70-71.

**9** Sicinski, Michael, "*A Separation* (Asghar Farhadi, Iran)," *Cinema Scope* 49, 2011, http://cinema-scope.com/currency/currency-a-separation-asghar-farhadi-iran/.

**10** Yong, William, "Iran Lifts Ban on Director, Saying He Issued an Apology," *The New York Times*, 2010, http://www.nytimes.com/2010/10/04/world/middleeast/04iran.html?_r=0.

**11** No author listed. "*A Separation* (2011)—Awards," *IMDb*, http://www.imdb.com/title/tt1832382/awards.

**12** No author listed. "*A Separation*," *Box Office Mojo*, http://www.boxofficemojo.com/movies/?page=main&id=aseperation.htm.

**13** Ebert, Roger, "The Best Films of 2011," *RogerEbert.com*, 2011, http://www.rogerebert.com/rogers-journal/the-best-films-of-2011.

## *The Past*

**1** Lodge, Guy, "Asghar Farhadi on Why *The Past* Is a Brother to *A Separation*," *HitFix*, 2013, http://www.hitfix.com/in-contention/interview-asghar-farhadi-on-why-the-past-is-a-brother-to-a-separation.

**2** Ibid.

**3** Roberts, Sheila, "Director Asghar Farhadi Talks *The Past*, His Inspiration for the Story, Filming a Different Side of Paris, the Oscar Controversy, and More," *Collider*, 2014, http://collider.com/asghar-farhadi-the-past-interview/.

4 Elsewhere, I've articulated my cases for the "Iranian" element in both *The Past* and Kiarostami's *Like Someone in Love* in two separate essays: "*The Past*: An Iranian in Paris," for *Guernica*, and "On the Alleged Decline of Iranian Cinema, and Why *Like Someone in Love* is an Iranian Film," on my personal website, http://tinahassannia.com/.

5 Farhadi, Asghar, Personal Interview (Part Two), T. Hassannia, August 3, 2014.

6 No author listed. "*The Past* (2014)—Awards," accessed July 24, 2014, http://www.imdb.com/title/tt2404461/awards.

7 Bradshaw, Peter, "*The Past* Review: 'Its Severity and Cerebral Force Are Beyond Question,'" *The Guardian*, 2014, http://www.theguardian.com/film/2014/mar/27/the-past-review-peter-bradshaw-asghar-farhadi.

8 D'Angelo, Mike, "*The Past* Is Another Emotionally Complex Triumph from Asghar Farhadi," *The A.V. Club*, 2013, http://www.avclub.com/review/the-past-is-another-emotionally-complex-triumph-fr-200679.

9 Sicinski, Michael, "Reviews of New Releases Seen from the Cannes 2013 Line-up," 2013, accessed July 13, 2014, http://academichack.net/reviews-Cannes2013.htm.

10 Lodge, Guy, "Asghar Farhadi on Why *The Past* Is a Brother to *A Separation*," *HitFix*, 2013, http://www.hitfix.com/in-contention/interview-asghar-farhadi-on-why-the-past-is-a-brother-to-a-separation.

# Bibliography

No author listed, "A Separation," *Box Office Mojo*, http://www.boxofficemojo.com/movies/?page=main&id=aseperation.htm.

No author listed, "A Separation (2011)—Awards," *IMDb*, http://www.imdb.com/title/tt1832382/awards.

No author listed, "About Elly (2009)—Awards," 2014, http://www.imdb.com/title/tt1360860/awards.

No author listed, "Asghar Farhadi's Iran," *Film Society of Lincoln Center*, http://www.filmlinc.com/films/series/asghar-farhadis-iran.

No author listed, "Asghar Farhadi, Oscar-Winning Iranian Director of *A Separation*, Says Next Film Will Be About PM Mohammad Mossadegh," *Melliun*, May 6, 2014, http://melliun.org/iran/40587.

No author listed, "Beautiful City (2004)—Awards," accessed July 1, 2014, http://www.imdb.com/title/tt0424434/awards?ref_=tt_ql_4.

No author listed, "Director Blames Media for Playing Up Movie Censorship in Iran," *Deutsche Welle*, 2009, http://www.dw.de/director-blames-media-for-playing-up-movie-censorship-in-iran/a-4010651.

No author listed, "Feature: Director's Commentary." *A Separation*, 2012, Sony Pictures Classic.

No author listed, "Fireworks Wednesday (2006)—Awards," accessed May 1, 2014, http://www.imdb.com/title/tt0845439/awards.

No author listed, "The Past (2014)—Awards," accessed July 24, 2014, http://www.imdb.com/title/tt2404461/awards.

No author listed, *Tabnak*, 2014, http://www.tabnak.ir/fa/news/418467/.

No author listed, "Tattered Lives in Divided Iran," *New York Review of Books*, 2011, http://www.nybooks.com/blogs/nyrblog/2011/sep/22/tattered-lives-divided-iran/.

No author listed, "Tribeca '09 Interview: *About Elly* Director Asghar Farhadi," World Narrative Feature Competition, *Indiewire*, http://www.indiewire.com/article/tribeca_09_interview_about_elly_director_asghar_farhadi_world_narrative_fea.

Blomfield, Bridget, "Fatimah," *Islamic Images and Ideas: Essays on Sacred Symbolism* (J. A. Morrow, McFarland & Company: 2013).

Bradshaw, Peter, "*Fireworks Wednesday*—Review," *The Guardian*, 2014, http://www.theguardian.com/film/2014/feb/06/fireworks-wednesday-review.

Bradshaw, Peter, "*The Past* Review: 'Its Severity and Cerebral Force Are Beyond Question,' " *The Guardian*, 2014, http://www.theguardian.com/film/2014/mar/27/the-past-review-peter-bradshaw-asghar-farhadi.

Burke, Joseph, "Rediscovering Morality Through Asghar Farhadi's *A Separation*," *Senses of Cinema*, 2011, http://sensesofcinema.com/2011/feature-articles/rediscovering-morality-through-ashgar-farhadi%E2%80%99s-a-separation/.

Cheshire, Godfrey, "*A Separation*: Scenes from a Marriage," *Film Comment*, 2013, http://www.filmcomment.com/article/scenes-from-a-marriage.

Concannon, Phil, "*About Elly*—Review," *Little White Lies*, 2012, http://www.littlewhitelies.co.uk/theatrical-reviews/about-elly-21838.

D'Angelo, Mike, "*The Past* Is Another Emotionally Complex Triumph from Asghar Farhadi," *The A.V. Club*, 2013, http://www.avclub.com/review/the-past-is-another-emotionally-complex-triumph-fr-200679.

Dabashi, Hamid, "The Tragic Endings of Iranian Cinema," *Aljazeera*, 2013, http://www.aljazeera.com/indepth/opinion/2013/03/2013320175739100357.html.

Dadar, Taraneh, "Melodrama in Post-Revolutionary Iranian Cinema," *Directory of World Cinema: Iran*, 2012. P. Jahed, *Intellect* 10, 143-147.

Ebert, Roger, "The Best Films of 2011," *RogerEbert.com*, 2011, http://www.rogerebert.com/rogers-journal/the-best-films-of-2011.

Ebert, Roger, "Good People Facing Impossible Questions," *RogerEbert.com*, 2011, http://www.rogerebert.com/interviews/good-people-facing-impossible-questions.

Farhadi, Asghar, Personal Interview (Part One), T. Hassannia, June 14, 2014.

Farhadi, Asghar, Personal Interview (Part Two), T. Hassannia, August 3, 2014.

Gamble, Patrick, "Film Review: *About Elly*," 2012, accessed July 19, 2014, http://www.cine-vue.com/2012/09/film-review-about-elly.html.

Gonzalez, Ed, "*Beautiful City*," *Slant Magazine*, 2006, http://www.slantmagazine.com/film/review/beautiful-city.

Hassannia, Tina, "On the Alleged Decline of Iranian Cinema, and Why *Like Someone in Love* is an Iranian Film," *Tumblr*, March 25, 2013, http://tinahassannia.tumblr.com/post/46229685236/on-the-alleged-decline-of-iranian-cinema-and-why-like.

Hassannia, Tina, "*The Past*: An Iranian in Paris," *Guernica*, December 20, 2013, http://www.guernicamag.com/daily/tina-hassannia-an-iranian-in-paris/.

Hinrichsen, Jens, "Elly . . . ," *Film-Dienst* 1, 2011, 29-30.

Jahed, Parviz, "Film of the Year: *About Elly*," *Directory of World Cinema: Iran*, 2012. P. Jahed, *Intellect* 10, 11-13.

Kasman, Daniel, "Tribeca 2009: *About Elly* (Farhadi, Iran)," MUBI Notebook, 2009, https://mubi.com/notebook/posts/tribeca-2009-about-elly-farhadi-iran.

Kemp, Philip, "Film of the Week: *About Elly*," *Sight & Sound*, http://www.bfi.org.uk/news-opinion/sight-sound-magazine/reviews-recommendations/film-week-about-elly.

Kern, Laura, "A Plea For Forgiveness Sweetens Intricate Twists And Turns of Justice in Iran," *The New York Times*, 2006, http://www.nytimes.com/2006/03/15/movies/15beau.html.

Lodge, Guy, "Asghar Farhadi on Why *The Past* Is a Brother to *A Separation*," *HitFix*, 2013, http://www.hitfix.com/in-contention/interview-asghar-farhadi-on-why-the-past-is-a-brother-to-a-separation.

Marsh, Calum, " 'I Don't Really Believe in Endings': An Interview with Iranian Director Asghar Farhadi," *Hazlitt*, 2014, http://www.randomhouse.ca/hazlitt/feature/i-dont-really-believe-endings-interview-iranian-director-asghar-farhadi.

Naficy, Hamid, *A Social History of Iranian Cinema*, Vol. 4 (Duke University Press: 2012), 251-261.

Nayman, Adam, "*A Separation*: Write Angles," *Reverse Shot*, 2011, http://www.reverseshot.com/article/separation.

Oleinik, Anton, "Dostoevsky's Journey to Iran," *CineAction* 90, 2013, http://www.questia.com/read/1G1-332396180.

O'Malley, Sheila, "...and Wednesday too: Asghar Farhadi's *Fireworks Wednesday*," *Slant Magazine*, 2007, http://www.slantmagazine.com/house/2007/30/and-wednesday-too-asghar-farhadis-fireworks-wednesday.

Price, Massoume, *Iran's Diverse Peoples: A Reference Sourcebook* (ABC-CLIO: 2005).

Rastin, Shadmehr, " 'Which part of this city is beautiful?'," *Film Monthly*, June 2004, Issue 318, 42-58.

Roberts, Sheila, "Director Asghar Farhadi Talks *The Past*, His Inspiration for the Story, Filming a Different Side of Paris, the Oscar Controversy, and More," *Collider*, 2014, http://collider.com/asghar-farhadi-the-past-interview/.

Saïd Amir Arjomand and Nathan J. Brown, *The Rule of Law, Islam, and Constitutional Politics in Egypt and Iran* (SUNY Press: 2013).

Scheib, Ronnie, "Review: *Beautiful City*," *Variety*, 2004, http://variety.com/2004/film/reviews/beautiful-city-1200530703/.

Sicinski, Michael, "*A Separation* (Asghar Farhadi, Iran)," *Cinema Scope* 49, 2011, http://cinema-scope.com/currency/currency-a-separation-asghar-farhadi-iran/.

Sicinski, Michael, "Reviews of New Releases Seen from the Cannes 2013 Line-up," 2013, accessed July 13, 2014, http://academichack.net/reviewsCannes2013.htm.

Simon, Alissa, "Review: *About Elly*," *Variety*, 2009, http://variety.com/2009/film/reviews/about-elly-1200473803/.

Smith, Damon, "Asghar Farhadi, *A Separation*," *Filmmaker Magazine*, 2011, http://filmmakermagazine.com/36713-asghar-farhadi-a-separation/.

Toossi, Javad, " 'Look at my tearful eyes,' " *Film Monthly*, March 2011, Issue 424, 70-71.

Tizro, Zahra, *Domestic Violence in Iran: Women, Marriage, and Islam* (Routledge: 2013).

Yong, William, "Iran Lifts Ban on Director, Saying He Issued an Apology," *The New York Times*, 2010, http://www.nytimes.com/2010/10/04/world/middleeast/04iran.html?_r=0.

Young, Deborah, "Review: *Fireworks Wednesday*," *Variety*, 2006, http://variety.com/2006/film/reviews/fireworks-wednesday-1200518706/.

# Index

*A Separation*, 3, 15, 21, 69-78
  Awards, 25-26
*About Elly*, 15, 21, 22, 54, 61-68
Alavi, Bozorg, 15
Beckett, Samuel, 8
Beizaei, Bahram, 7
*Beautiful City*, 20-21, 23-24, 39-48
*Blind Owl, The*, 7
Bradshaw, Peter, 53, 83
Burke, Joseph, 1, 3
Censorship, 16-18
Chadors, 57-59
Cheshire, Godfrey, 73
Chekhov, Anton, 7
Chubak, Sadeq, 15
Concannon, Phil, 64-65
Dabashi, Hamid, 2-3
*Dancing in the Dust*, 3, 11, 12-14, 19, 20-21, 29-37, 52
D'Angelo, Mike, 83
*Diyat*, 42
Dolatabadi, Mahmoud, 7, 15
Dostoevsky, Fyodor, 3-4
*Dumb Waiter, The*, 8
Ebert, Roger, 72, 77
*Eyes*, 9
Fajr International Film Festival, 28, 41, 53
Farhadi, Asghar
  Early cinema experiences, 11-12
  Family, 26
  Life, 2-3
  Radio, 9-10
  Television, 10-11
  Theater, 6-7, 9

Farzanehpur, Dana, 82
Field, Syd, 15
Filmmaking in Europe, 24-25
*Fireworks Wednesday* (Film), 14, 15, 19, 22, 49-59
Fireworks Wednesday (Holiday), 52
Gamble, Patrick, 63
Gonzalez, Ed, 41
Haghighi, Mani, 50-51
Hedayat, Sadegh, 15
*HitFix*, 81
Ibsen, Henrik, 7
Ionesco, Eugene, 7
Iranian Legal System, 42, 46
Islamic Republic of Iran Broadcasting, 2
Jahed, Parviz, 63
Javanmard, Abbas, 10
Kalari, Mahmoud, 81
Kanun, 9n3
Karimi, Nosrat, 14
Kemp, Philip, 64
Kern, Laura, 41
Khodabendeh, Nogole, 82
Kiarostami, Abbas, 1, 82
Leigh, Mike, 21
*Low Heights*, 3
Makhmalbaf, Mohsen, 1, 77
Marriage, 13, 27, 31, 33
Ministry of Culture and Islamic Guidance, 17
Mosaddegh, Mohammad, 5-6
Naficy, Hamid, 2n3
Naraghi, Maryam, 82
Nazari, Nassime, 82
Nayman, Adam, 73

*New York Review of Books, The*, 71
O'Malley, Sheila, 56
Panahi, Jafar, 1, 77
*Past, The*, 19-20, 21, 23, 24, 43, 79-87
Pinter, Harold, 7-8
*Qesas*, 42
Radin, Manouchehr, 7
*Radio*, 8
*Report, The*, 54n9
Saedi, Gholam-Hossein, 7
Safiyari, Hayedeh, 25, 71, 81
Scheib, Ronnie, 41
Shakespeare, William, 7
*Shahnameh*, 30, 86
Sicinski, Michael, 3, 77, 84
Simon, Alissa, 63
Taghipour, Iraj, 40
*Tale of a City*, 2, 10
Tarbiat Modarres University, 2
Toossi, Javad, 76
Toussi, Farhad Taghizadeh, 82
Welfling, Juliette, 81
*White Balloon, The*, 77
Williams, Tennessee, 7
Young, Deborah, 53
Young Iranian Cinema Society, 2, 8-9
Zahra, Fatima, 45

## About the Author

Tina Hassannia is a film critic and writer. Her work has appeared in *The Guardian, The Globe and Mail, Slant Magazine, Reverse Shot, Maisonneuve, Guernica, Little White Lies, Keyframe, Grolsch Film Works,* and others. She is the co-host of *Hello Cinema,* a podcast dedicated to Iranian cinema. She was born in Tehran and lives in Toronto, Canada. You can find her online at tinahassannia.com.